Let's Investigate

Handling Data 3

Written by Beryl Webber & Jean Haigh

Published by Scholastic Publications Ltd,
Marlborough House, Holly Walk,
Leamington Spa, Warwickshire CV32 4LS

Written by Jean Haigh and Beryl Webber
Edited by Jackie Cunningham-Craig
Series designed by Sue Limb
Illustrated by Chris Saunderson

Designed using Aldus Pagemaker
Processed by Studio Photoset, Leicester
Artwork by Norfolk House Graphic Designers,
Leicester
Printed in Great Britain by Pindar Print,
Scarborough

© 1990 Scholastic Publications Ltd.

British Library Cataloguing in Publication Data
Webber, Beryl
      Let's investigate handling data.
      3.
      1. Mathematics
      I. Title II. Haigh, Jean
      510

ISBN 0 590 76233 8

Front and back cover: photographs by Martyn
Chillmaid, designed by Sue Limb

Contents

About the series

Learning mathematics is a creative activity. This is as equally true for today's children as it was for Sir Isaac Newton. All learners explore the wealth of mathematical achievement, creatively putting their own stamp upon it and making it unique for them. For example the child who begins to have an awareness of infinity is personally recreating ideas that are part of our mathematical inheritance but which cannot be directly taught. The learner draws upon a wide variety of experiences and ultimately combines them to form a unique and personal notion of infinity.

But as we live in a social environment each individual needs to be able to communicate their own personal mathematics to a wider audience. Newton's mathematical principles would have been lost forever when he died had he not used some conventions to communicate his ideas. We all must follow conventions if we intend to share our mathematics with others.

'Mathematics is not just about number and shape, it can be said to happen whenever the mind classifies and creates structures.' (Notes on *Mathematics in Primary Schools*, 1967)

This definition, written by members of the Association of Teachers of Mathematics, is as relevant today as it was more than 20 years ago. Investigative mathematics is a way of allowing children to become independent mathematical thinkers. Children who have the opportunity to experience mathematics in a variety of situations and who successfully face challenges are able to use their energy and enthusiasm to become creative mathematicians.

This philosophy is central to our thinking and underpins the *Let's Investigate* series. We hope that these books will provide useful resources and ideas for you to use in the classroom in order to give children some opportunities to explore the richness of mathematics. We have deliberately not structured the series to form a mathematics scheme or programme. It is a collection of ideas to be dipped into to support the children's learning. The activities are not necessarily arranged in any order of difficulty but attempt to open children's eyes to the awe and wonder of mathematics.

We both hope you will find this series a useful and enjoyable classroom resource to share with your children.

Jean Haigh
Beryl Webber

Introduction

Each topic in the series consists of three books: Book 1 which is aimed at approximately the six- to eight-year-old age range, Book 2 for the eight- to ten-year-old and Book 3 for children aged ten to twelve years. We feel that photocopiable pages are inappropriate for the very youngest children in school and so Book 1 is only suitable for children who have had some time to explore their classroom environment and to develop some basic manipulative skills.

We have chosen handling data for the fourth topic in the series because it is fundamental to the mathematical learning of young children. This is reflected in the National Curriculum.

All the activities are exploratory, but due to the nature of the topic, they all have defined parameters. In forming the activities we have taken note of the Attainment Targets of the National Curriculum, focusing on Levels 3 to 5 for Book 3. Most of the activities have ideas for further investigation.

The activities are all embedded in situations that will be familiar to the children. They are, however, necessarily based on fictional information. We feel that, as the children mature mathematically, they should be encouraged to collect, represent and interpret their own data. Our intention for Book 3 is for the children to become familiar and confident with the collection, handling, representation and interpretation of data. They are progressively introduced to the language associated with the various forms of graphical representation.

The teachers' instructions in each book follow a similar format and the objectives are stated clearly. We have designed the illustrations on the photocopiable pages to be clear, easy-to-handle and motivational for young children.

The photocopiable pages are resource sheets that can be used with individuals, pairs or groups of children. We hope that the ideas will be extended by you and your pupils and that the resource sheets will be developed and used in other ways.

The teachers' instructions include many questions which either you or your pupils may raise. The children should be encouraged to pose and explore their own personal questions. The representation of data is only valid if sensible interpretations can be made.

Mathematical skills

Measuring accurately, use 24 hour and 12 hour time, tabulations, hypothesising, predicting, relate variables, classify objects, use money, multiplication and subtraction, use ratio and proportion.

Materials

Most of the activities require pencils. Some require dice, coloured pencils, thin card, scissors and adhesive. A calculator would be useful for some activities.

Collecting & classifying

Early morning

See photocopiable pages 9 and 10.

Objective

To place activities in sequence into a simple linear flow diagram.

Classroom development

Cut out the five pictures from page 9. Place them in time sequence on the flow diagram on page 10. Compare your sequence with a friend's. Are there any differences? Is it possible to have any other sequence? What activities could go before and after those provided?

Draw pictures or write sentences, in the blank spaces on page 9, that describe a sequence of activities. Cut them out and ask a friend to place them on the flow diagram. Discuss the sequence your friend has chosen. Stick the pictures on to the flow diagram.

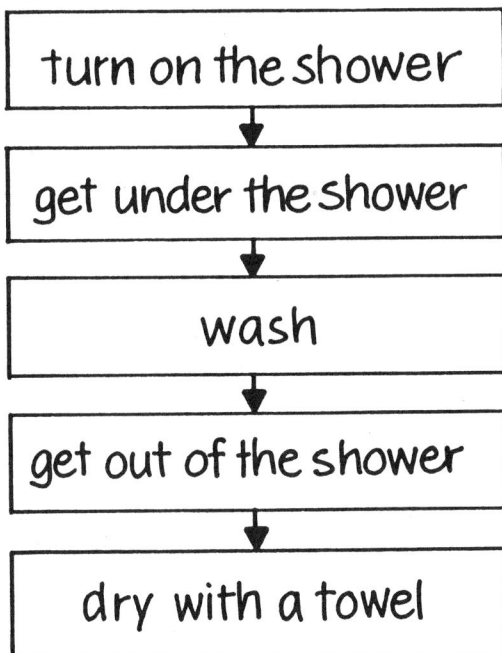

```
┌─────────────────────────────┐
│   turn on the shower        │
└─────────────────────────────┘
              ↓
┌─────────────────────────────┐
│   get under the shower      │
└─────────────────────────────┘
              ↓
┌─────────────────────────────┐
│           wash              │
└─────────────────────────────┘
              ↓
┌─────────────────────────────┐
│   get out of the shower     │
└─────────────────────────────┘
              ↓
┌─────────────────────────────┐
│    dry with a towel         │
└─────────────────────────────┘
```

Further activities

Write clear instructions for using a school electrical appliance eg a video or a projector. Put them into a flow diagram format. Keep them with the machine to help unfamiliar users.

Evening activities

See photocopiable pages 11 and 12.

Objective

To place activities in sequence in a flow diagram with decision boxes.

Classroom development

Cut out the pictures and the completed decision boxes on page 11. Place them in time sequence on the flow diagram on page 12. Decide first, where the decision boxes should be placed. Compare your flow diagram with a friend's. How many different but sensible flow diagrams can you make?

Draw pictures or write sentences, in the blank spaces on page 11 that describe a sequence of activities with two decisions. Cut them out and ask a friend to place them on the diagram. Discuss the sequence with your friend and then stick the pictures on to the flow diagram.

Further activities

Write clear instructions for crossing a busy road. Put them into a flow diagram using some decision boxes.

Naming quadrilaterals

See photocopiable pages 13 and 14.

Objective

To use a key to name quadrilaterals.

Classroom development

Cut out the quadrilaterals on page 13. Look at them carefully and identify their properties eg equal sides, parallel sides, right angles.

Use the key on page 14 to discover the correct names of the quadrilaterals by passing each shape through the successive stages of the key. Write the name on each shape. What can you say about each shape? What is the relationship between the square and the rhombus, and between the parallelogram and the rectangle?

Further activities

Find and identify, using reference books, six leaves or six mini-beasts. Write a key to sort them out. Ask a friend to name your items using your key.

Quadrilaterals

See photocopiable pages 13 to 15.

Objective

To classify certain quadrilaterals using inclusions.

Classroom development

Identify the square, rectangle, rhombus and parallelogram from page 13 and cut them out. Place them inside the outer boundary on page 15.

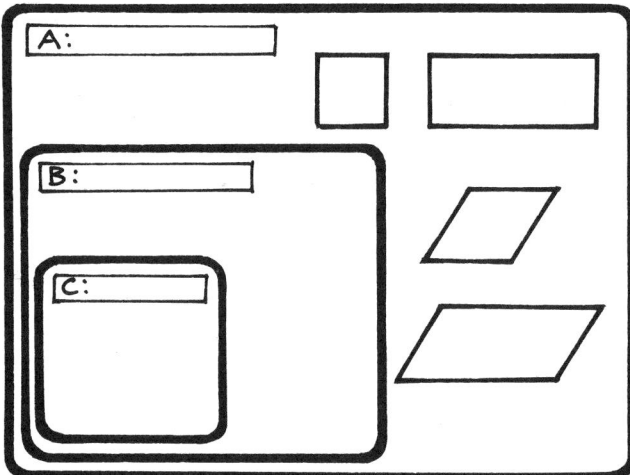

Move those shapes with right angles into the middle sector of the diagram.

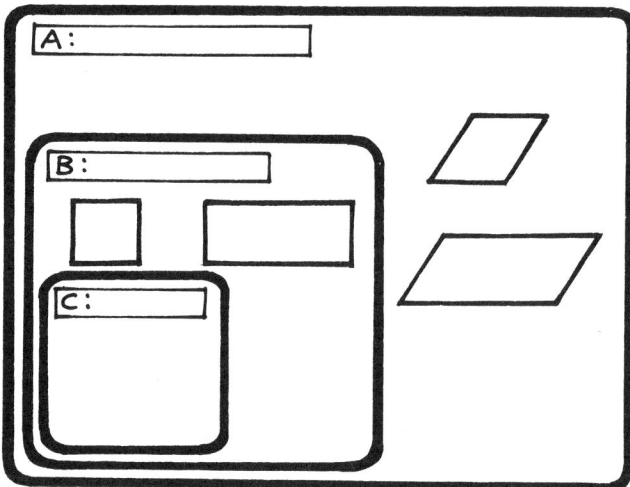

Move the shape with four equal sides into the centre sector.

Identify appropriate labels for each area. What can you say about the square? Which shapes on the diagrams could be called rectangles?

Move all the shapes back to the outer area of the diagram. Move those shapes with four equal sides to the middle sector and then the shape with right angles to the centre.

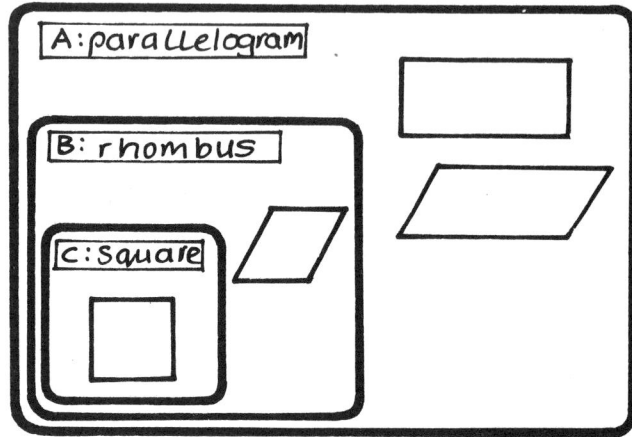

Identify appropriate labels. What can you say about the square? Which shapes on the diagram could be called rhombuses?

How many different but correct names could a square have?

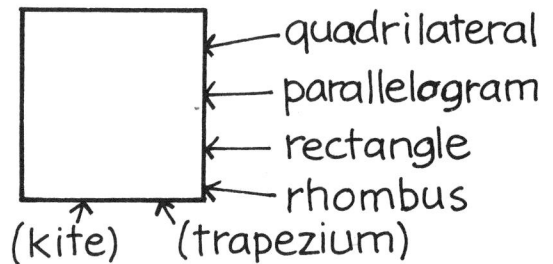

How many different names can you find for a rhombus?

Further activity

Find or draw pictures of a woman, a man, a boy and a girl. Use the diagram on page 15 to sort them out. How many different ways can this be done?

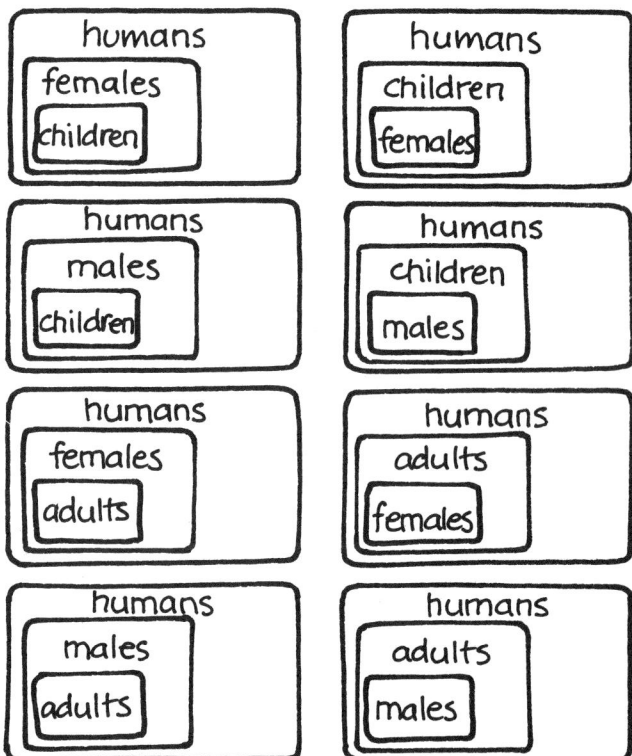

Early morning

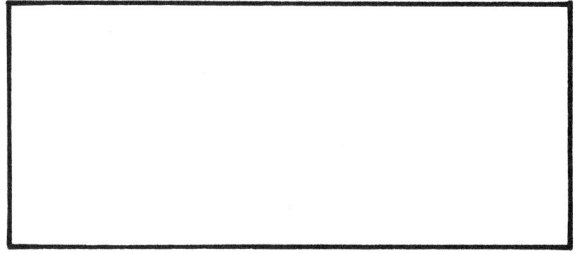

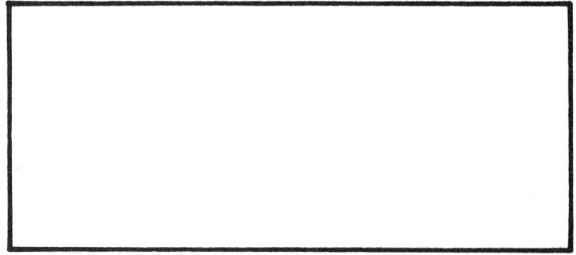

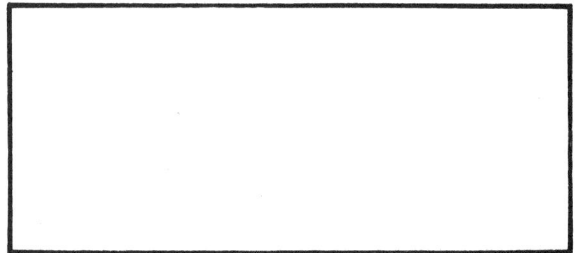

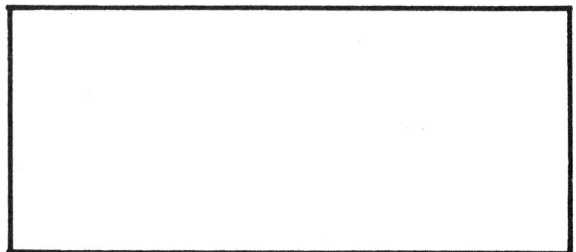

Early morning

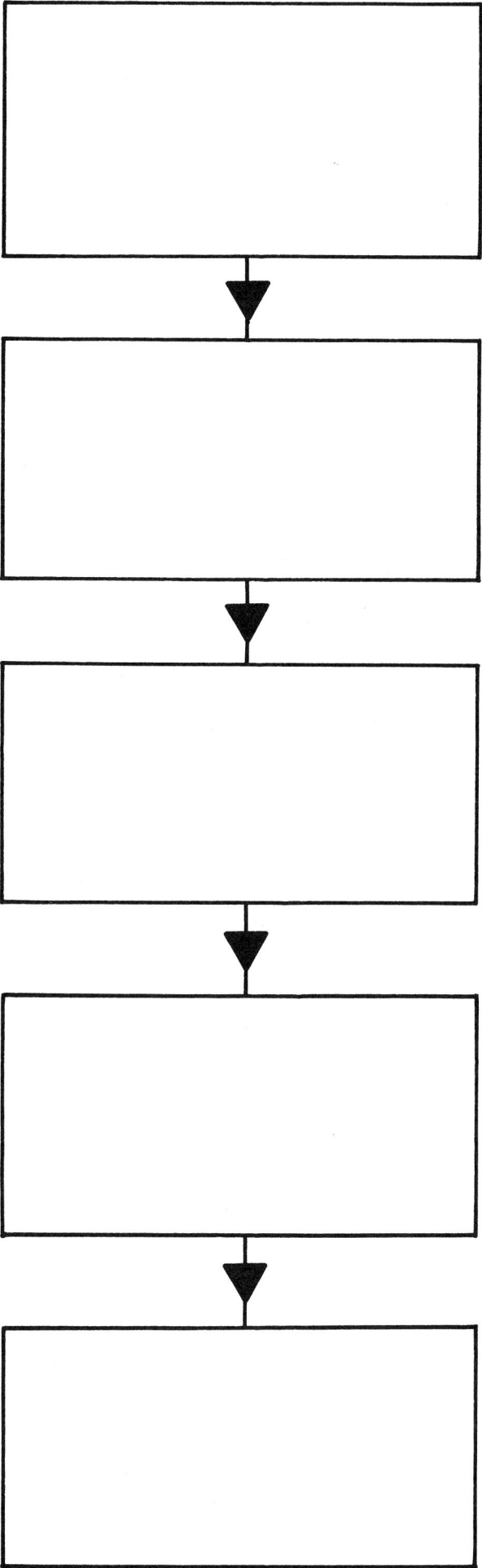

Evening activities

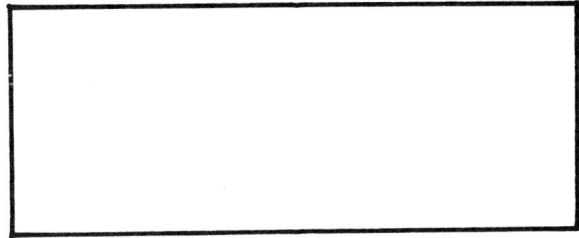

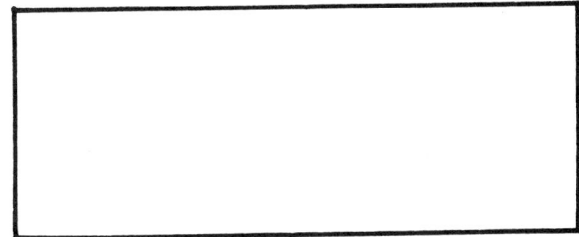

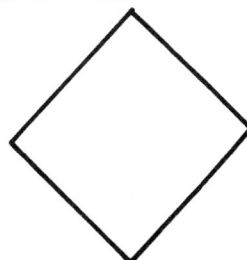

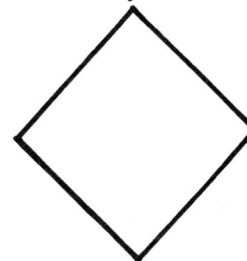

11

Evening activities

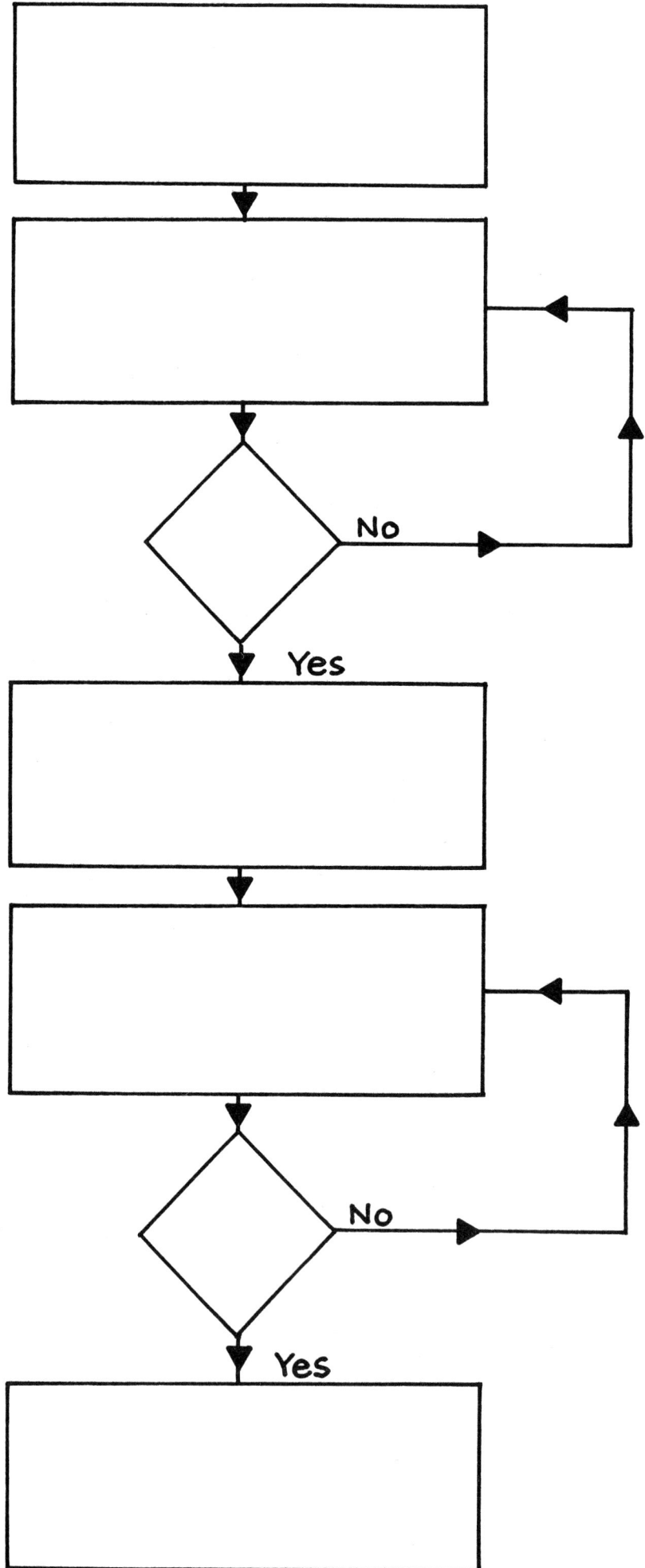

Naming quadrilaterals

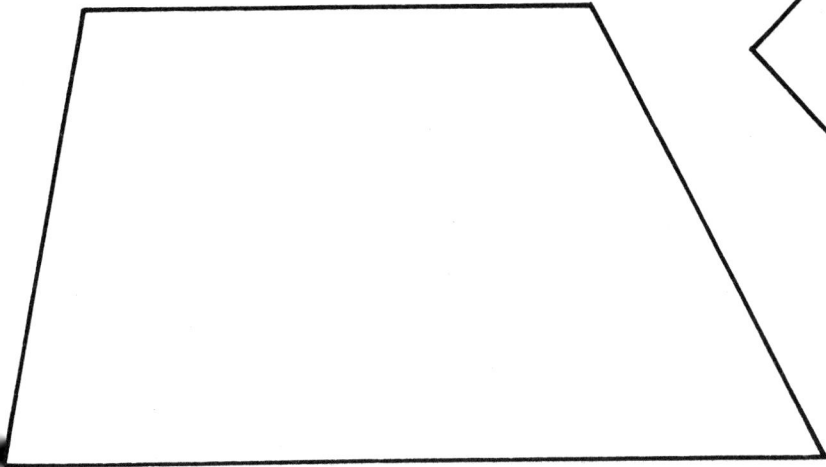

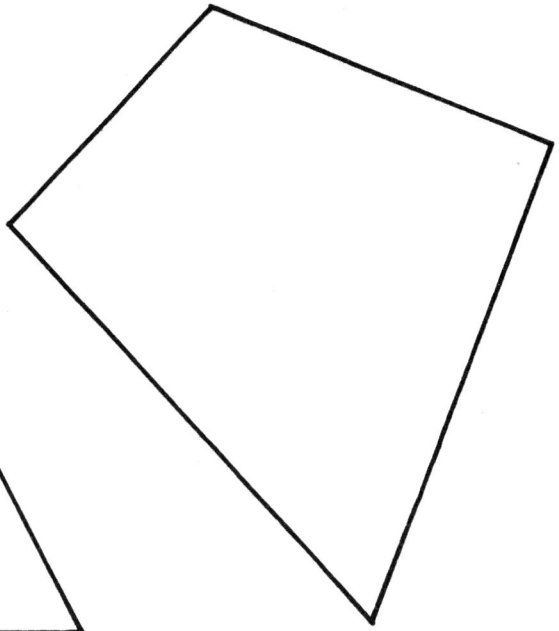

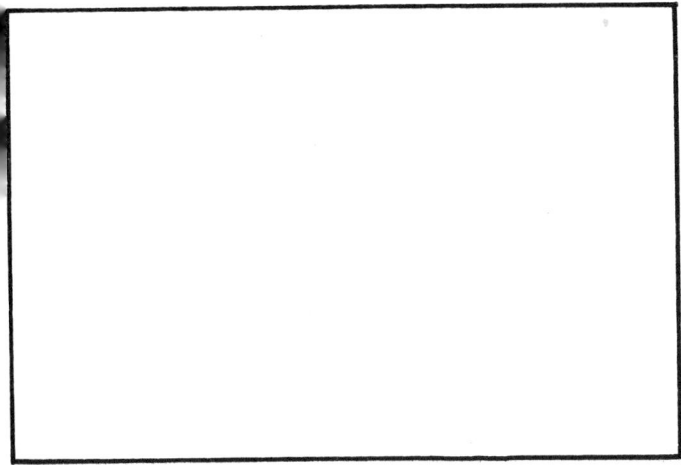

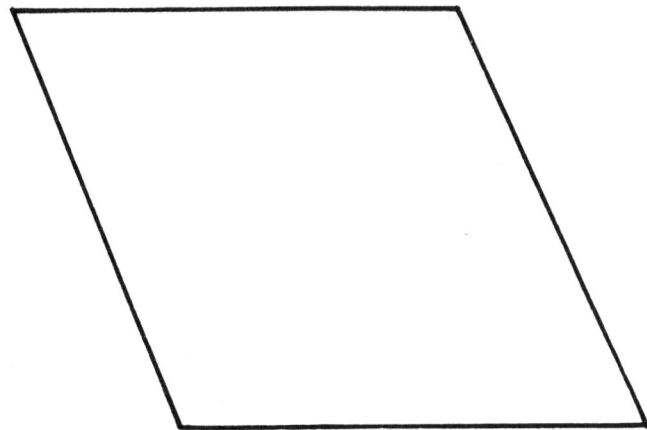

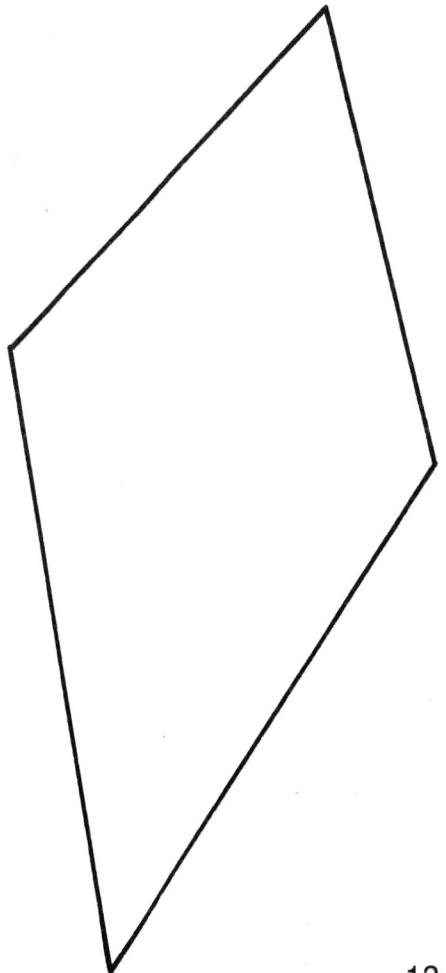

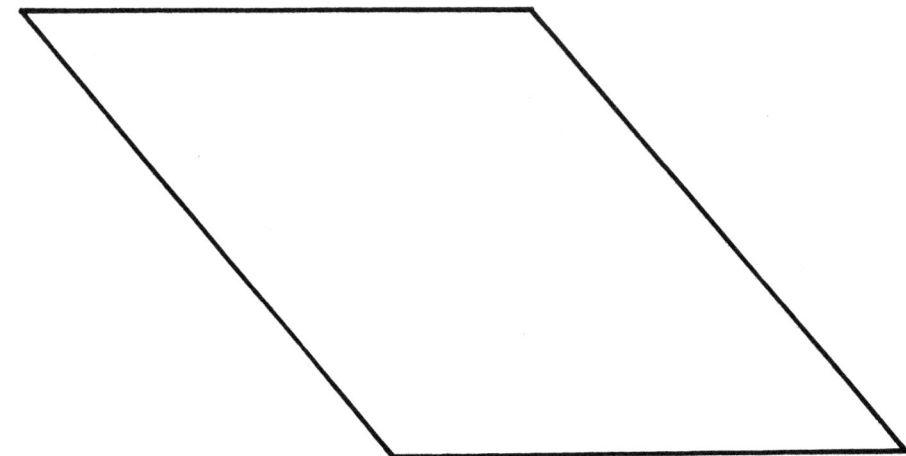

Naming quadrilaterals

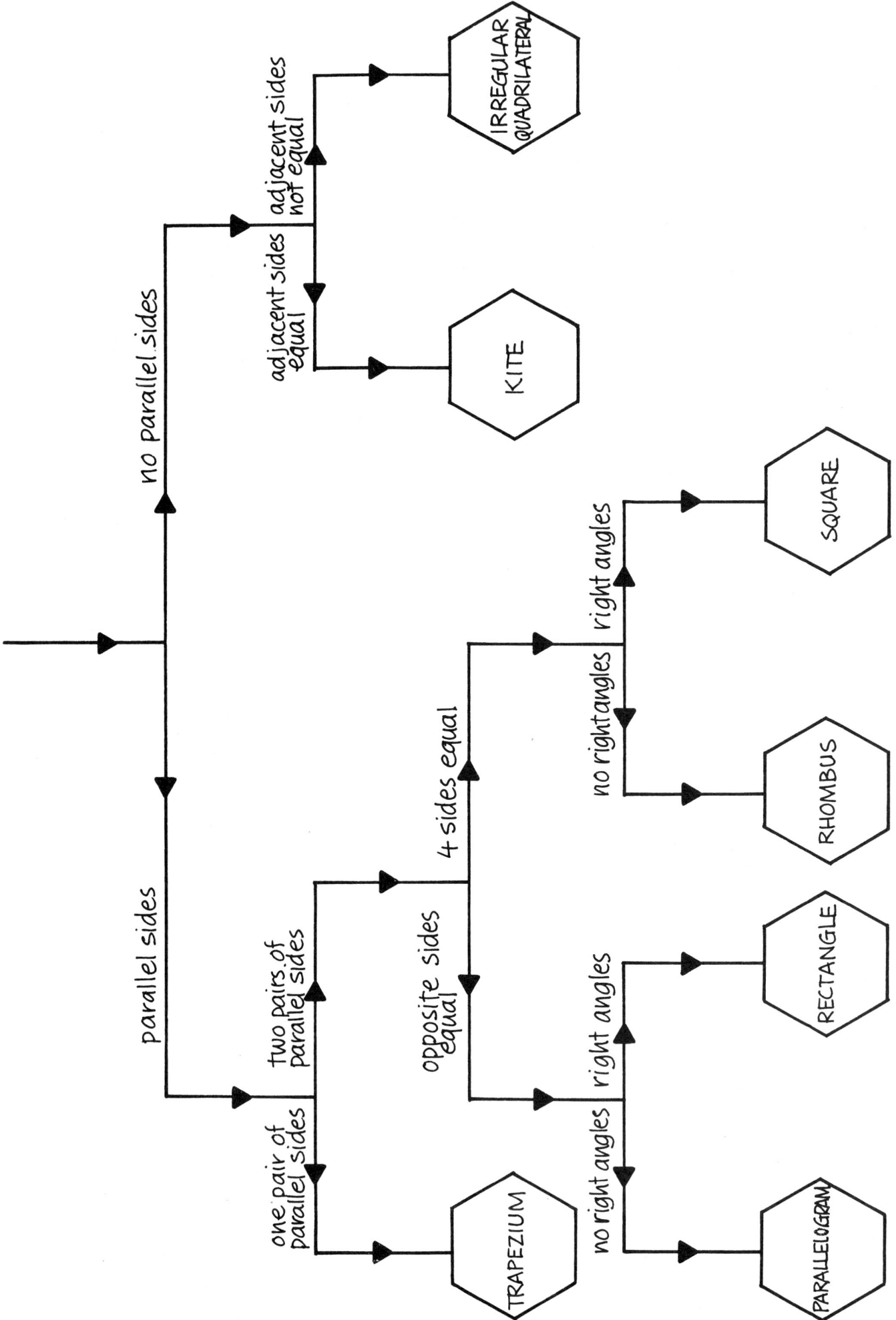

A flowchart for naming quadrilaterals:

- **no parallel sides**
  - **adjacent sides not equal** → IRREGULAR QUADRILATERAL
  - **adjacent sides equal** → KITE
- **parallel sides**
  - **one pair of parallel sides** → TRAPEZIUM
  - **two pairs of parallel sides**
    - **opposite sides equal**
      - **no right angles** → PARALLELOGRAM
      - **right angles** → RECTANGLE
    - **4 sides equal**
      - **no right angles** → RHOMBUS
      - **right angles** → SQUARE

Quadrilaterals

A:

B:

C:

Organising

Hands and feet

See photocopiable pages 19.

Objective

To collect data, and to form a scatter diagram using continuous variables.

Classroom development

Measure the distance of your hand span.

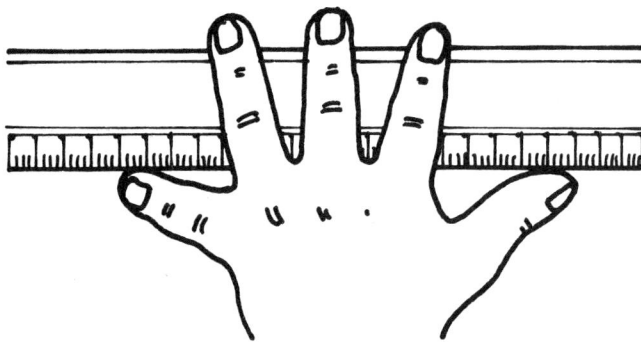

Measure the length of your foot.

Mark your results on the scatter diagram on page 19 by placing a cross at the appropriate point on the grid.

Collect the equivalent measurements from several friends and record their results on the diagram. Look at the distribution of the crosses. Can you draw any conclusions? Do most people who have small feet have short hand spans? Do most people who have long hand spans also have big feet? Is there anyone who has large feet and a short hand span or vice-versa?

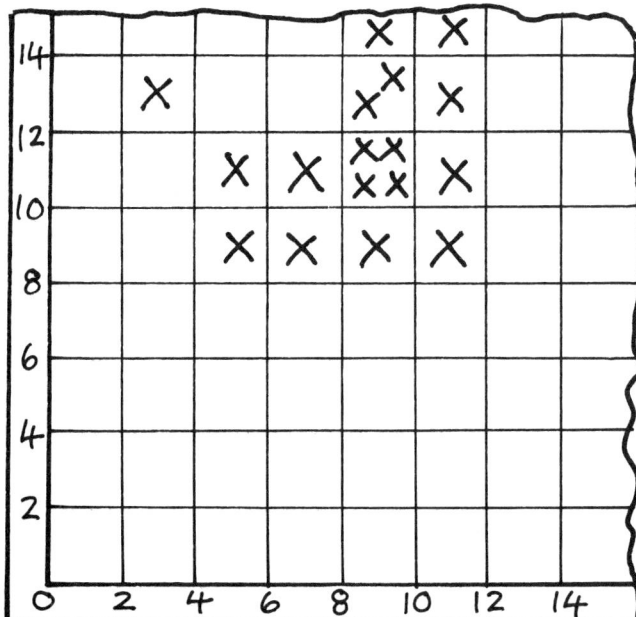

Quick work

See photocopiable pages 20 and 21.

Objective

To collect data to form a scatter diagram using continuous variables.

Classroom development

Ask a friend to time you while you add the till receipt on page 20 using a calculator. Record how long you took. Now ask your friend to time you completing the picture on page 20.

Mark your results on the scatter diagram on page 21 by placing a cross at the appropriate point on the grid.

Collect the times of several friends and record their results on the diagram.

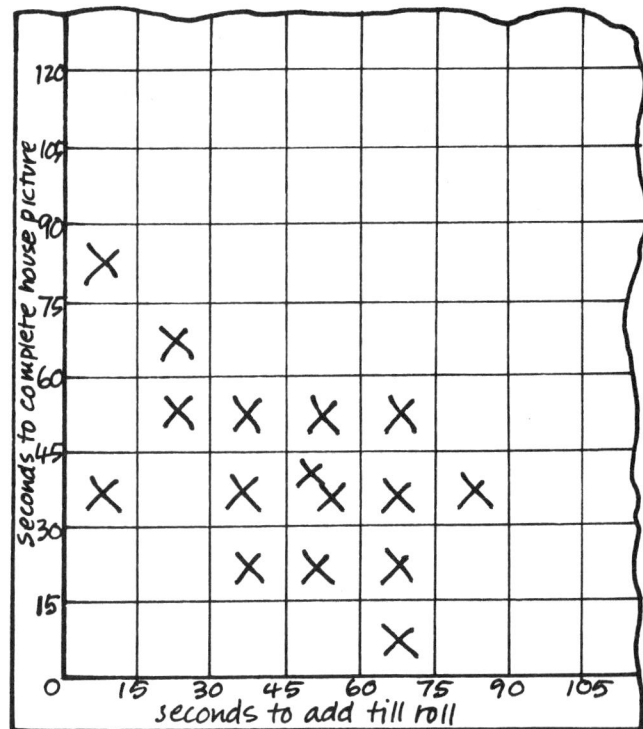

Look at the distribution of crosses. Can you draw any conclusions? Were most people quick at both tasks or slow at both tasks? Were there some people who were speedy at one task but quite slow at the other?

Further activities

Collect two sets of data about a group of people eg height and the time they get up in the morning or length of arm and height of standing jump. Is there any relationship between the two sets of data?

Pocket money

See photocopiable pages 22 and 23.

Objective

To collect continuous data using class intervals, and to create a frequency diagram.

Classroom development

Take a survey of pocket money in your school. If possible ask at least 50 people from four classes in your school. Record the data on the frequency table on page 22 using a different colour for each class in the school.

Record pocket money up to, but not including £1 in the first row. Record amounts from £1 up to, but not including £2 in the second row and so on. Record pocket money of £10 and over in the last row. For example:

	CLASS INTERVAL	TALLY	TOTAL
95p →	$m < £1·00$	I	
£1·00 →	$£1·00 \leqslant m < £2·00$	I	
2·99 →	$£2·00 \leqslant m < £3·00$	I	
3·00 →	$£3·00 \leqslant m < £4·00$	I	
4·50 →	$£4·00 \leqslant m < £5·00$	I	
	$£5·00 \leqslant m < £6·00$	I	

Total the tallies and use the data to draw a frequency diagram. Put the information from the first row of the table into the first column of the diagram. Continue in this way until the diagram is complete.

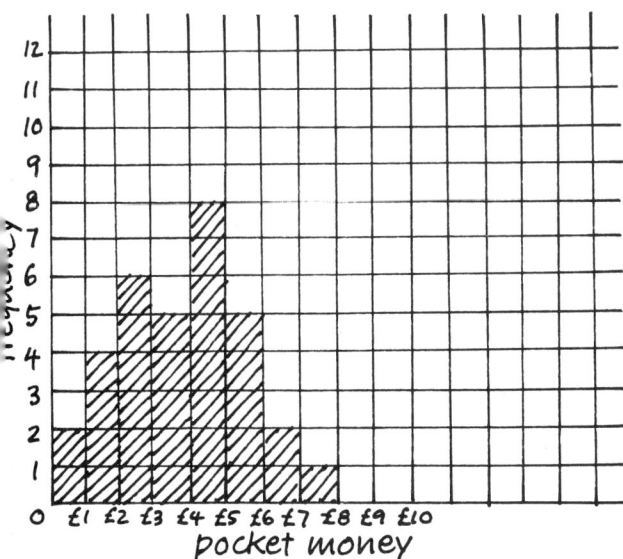

pocket money

Which interval of pocket money is the most common? Calculate the mean pocket money by multiplying the number of people per interval by the mid point of the interval. For example:

$$6 \times £2·50 = £15·00$$

Repeat for every interval, total the answers and divide by the number of people you surveyed.

Mark the mean on the frequency diagram. Compare the number of people who receive more than the mean pocket money with those who receive less. Can you explain any difference there might be?

Calculate separate means for each class you surveyed. Record them on a table. For example:

class	mean	range
1	£1·59	
2	£2·25	
3	£2·89	
4	£3·42	

Find the range of pocket money for each class by subtracting the lowest amount from the highest amount.

Which class has the highest mean pocket money? Do younger pupils usually receive less pocket money?

Further activities

Take a survey of the amount of time it takes pupils to reach your school.

Use class intervals to help you record your data. Draw a frequency diagram and calculate the mean and the range of the journey times.

The High Street

See photocopiable pages 24 to 27.

Objective

To draw pie charts to show collected data.

Classroom development

Look at the picture on page 24. Count the numbers of each type of animal shown. How many animals are there altogether?

Choose a colour to represent each species of animal and record this in the key beside the pie chart at the top of page 25.

Colour one section for each animal in the picture. Group together the sections in each colour. Complete the dotted line round each section. For example:

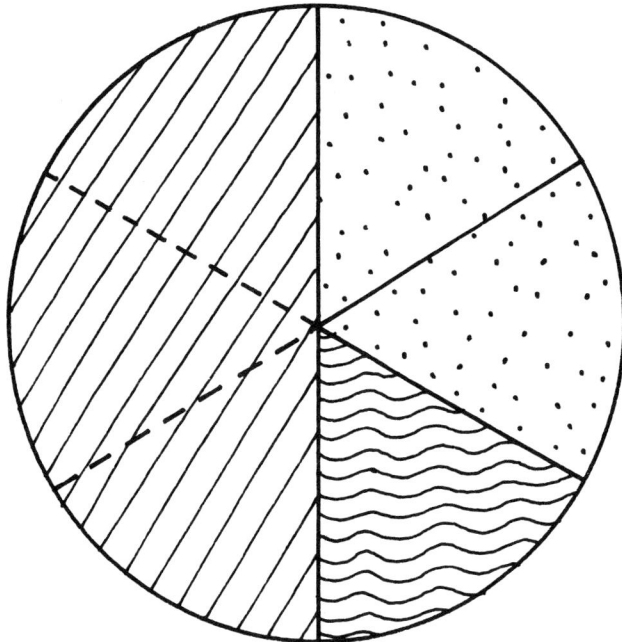

What proportion of the animals are cats? What proportion of the animals are dogs?

Look again at the picture on page 24. Make a survey of the traffic shown. Complete the pie chart on the bottom of page 25 as previously.

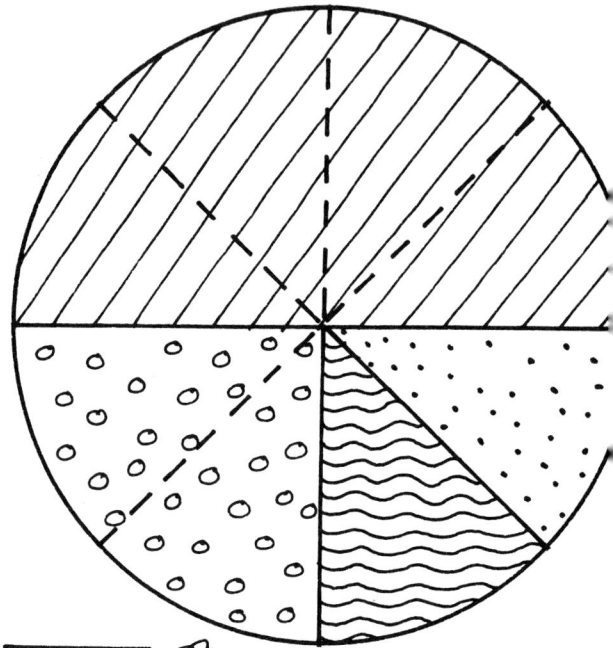

What proportion of the traffic is cars? What proportion of the traffic is lorries?

Further activities

Ask 12 friends to say which season their birthdays are in. Record this information on the pie chart on page 26.

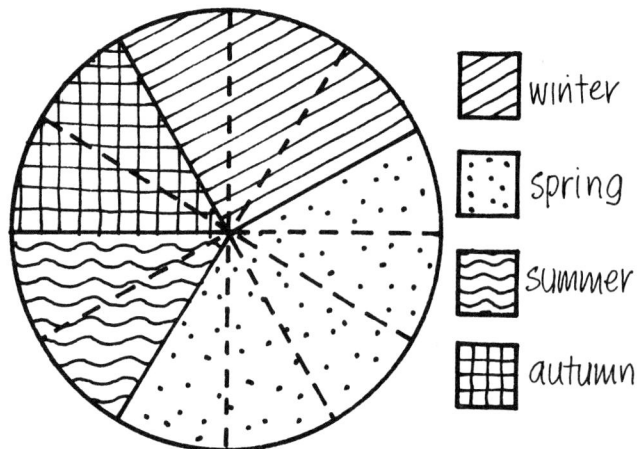

A pie chart to show what season we were born in

Which season is the most common to be born in?

Keep a diary of your activities on one 24 hour day. Record this data on the pie chart on page 27.

Hand and feet

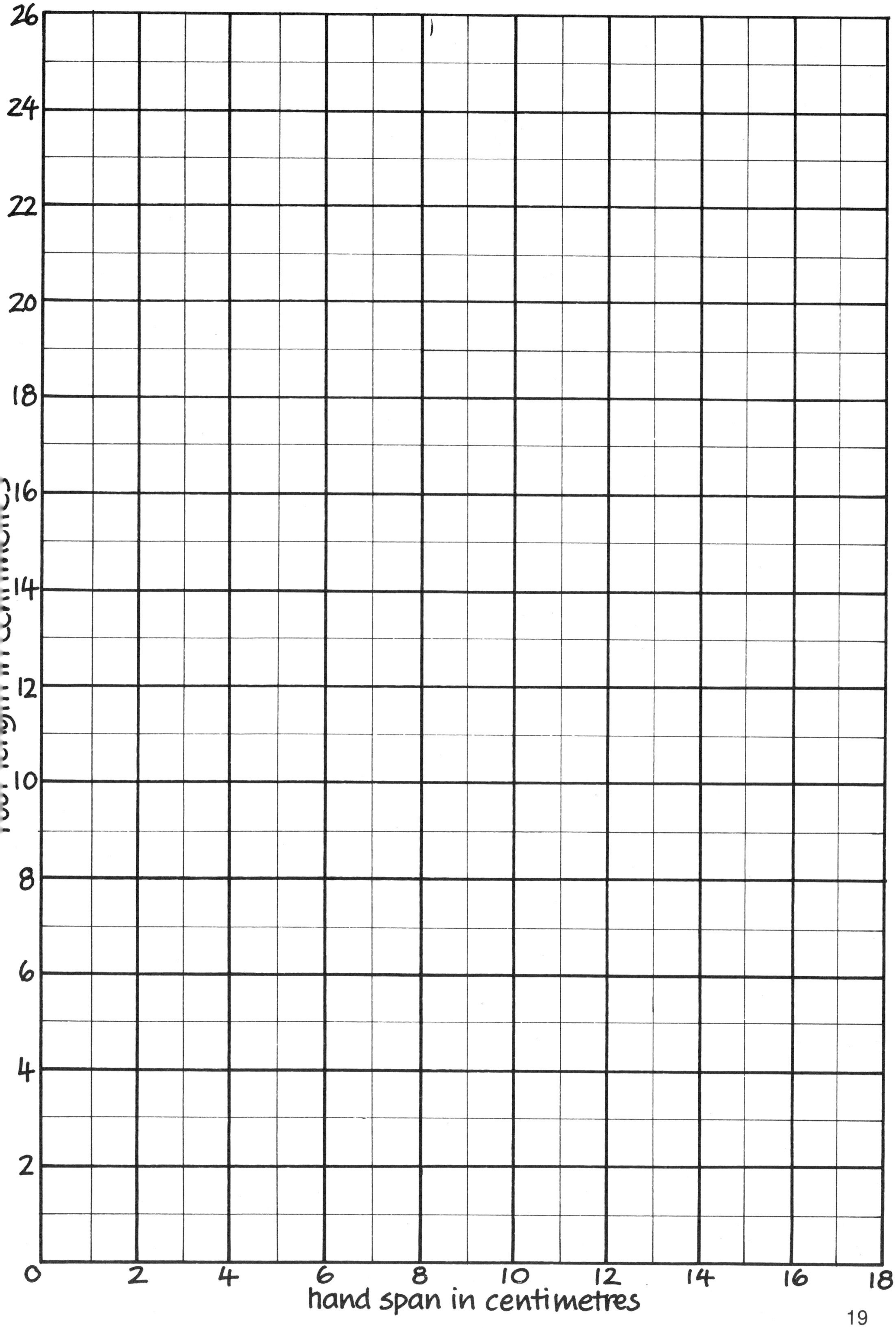

Quick work

SUPERSTORES

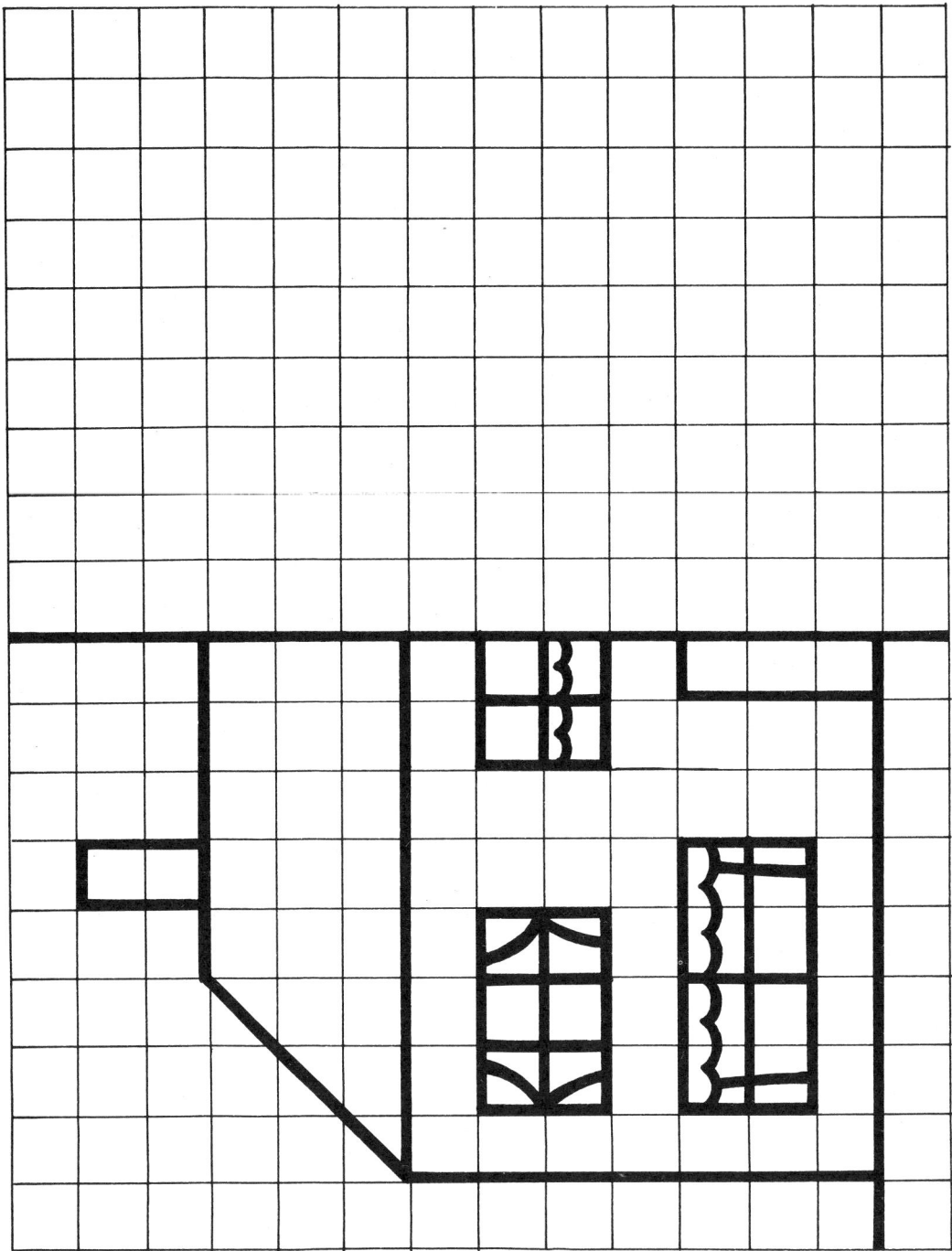

MEAT	1.20
VEG.	.40
VEG.	.25
COFFEE	.99
PROV.	1.39
MISC.	2.99
PROV.	.23
PROV.	.23
MEAT	3.51
VEG.	1.04
MISC.	2.79
FROZ.	1.11
FROZ.	.75
VEG.	.60
CONFEC.	.18
TOTAL	
DATE	TIME

Quick work

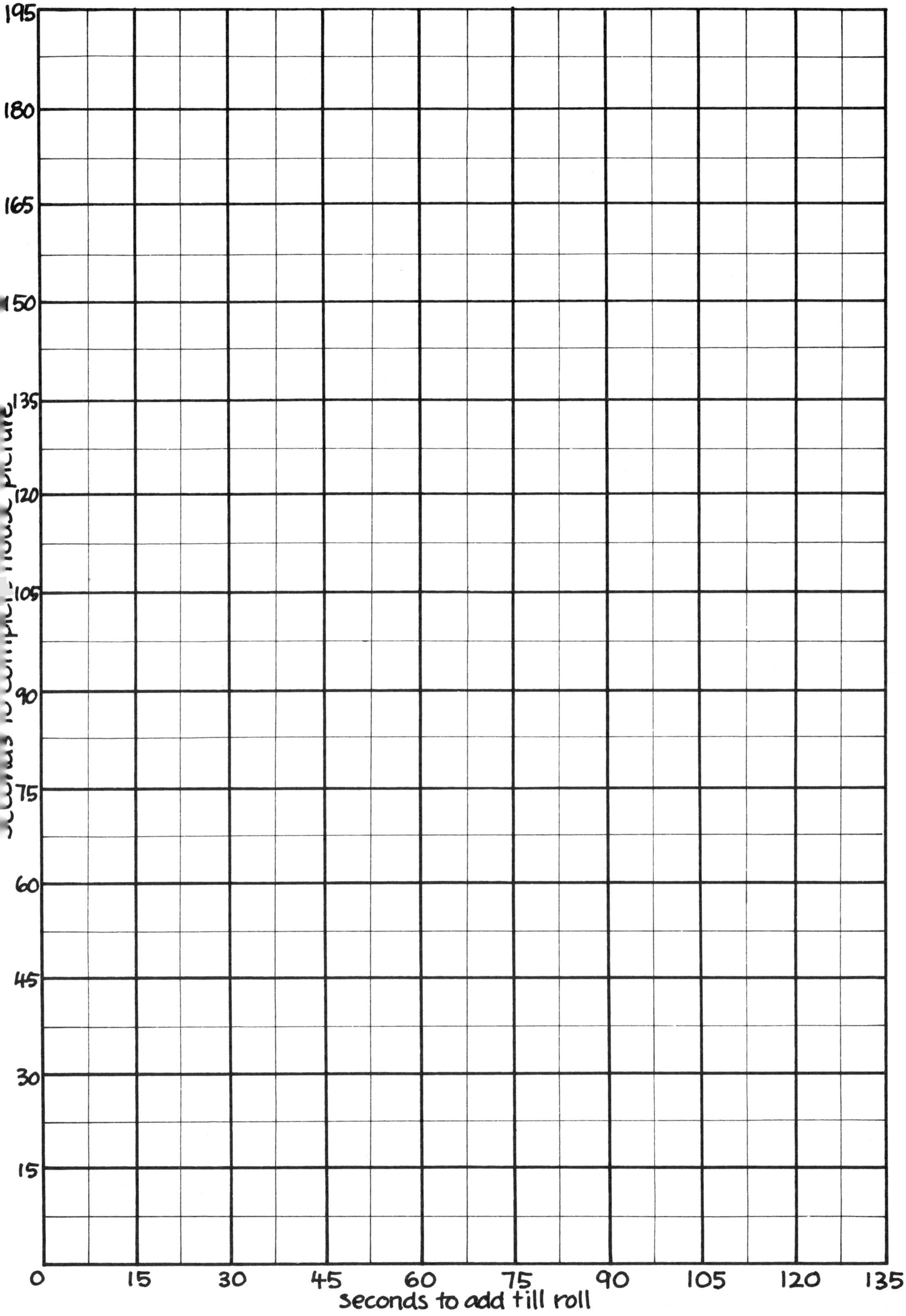
195
180
165
150
135
120
105
90
75
60
45
30
15
0
15
30
45
60
75
90
105
120
135
seconds to add till roll

Pocket money

CLASS INTERVAL	TALLY	TOTAL
$m < £1.00$		
$£1.00 \leqslant m < £2.00$		
$£2.00 \leqslant m < £3.00$		
$£3.00 \leqslant m < £4.00$		
$£4.00 \leqslant m < £5.00$		
$£5.00 \leqslant m < £6.00$		
$£6.00 \leqslant m < £7.00$		
$£7.00 \leqslant m < £8.00$		
$£8.00 \leqslant m < £9.00$		
$£9.00 \leqslant m < £10.00$		
$£10.00 \leqslant m$		

Pocket money

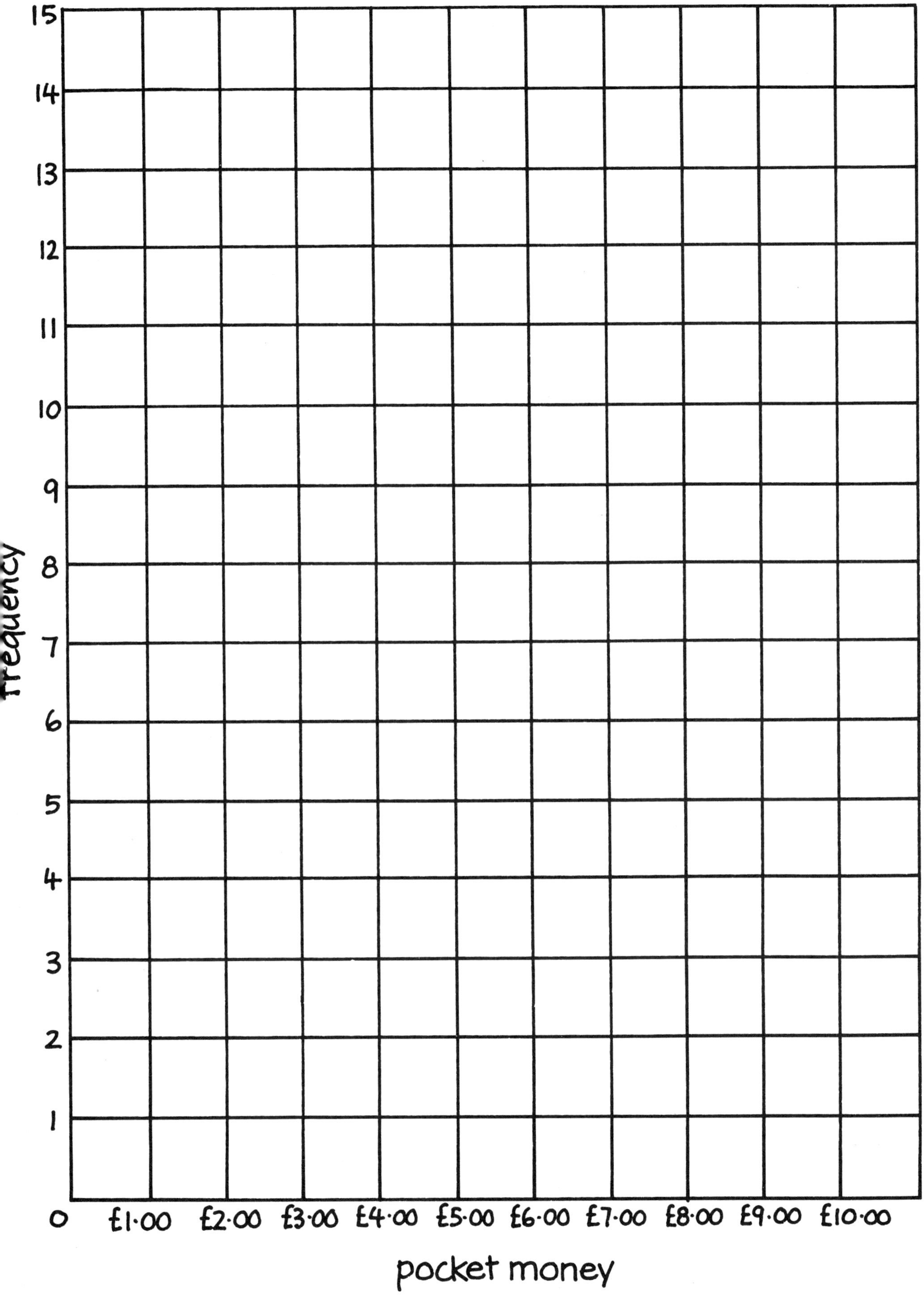

15
14
13
12
11
10
9
8
7
6
5
4
3
2
1
0
£1·00
£2·00
£3·00
£4·00
£5·00
£6·00
£7·00
£8·00
£9·00
£10·00
pocket money

The High Street

The High Street

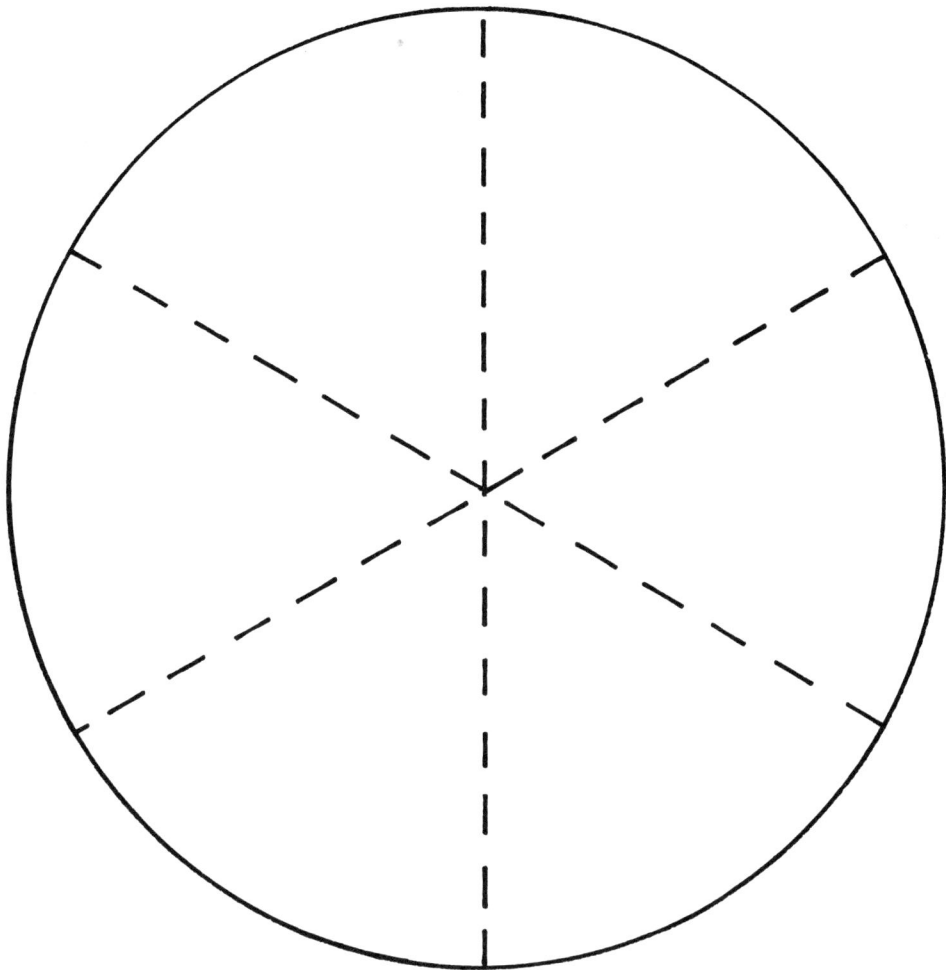

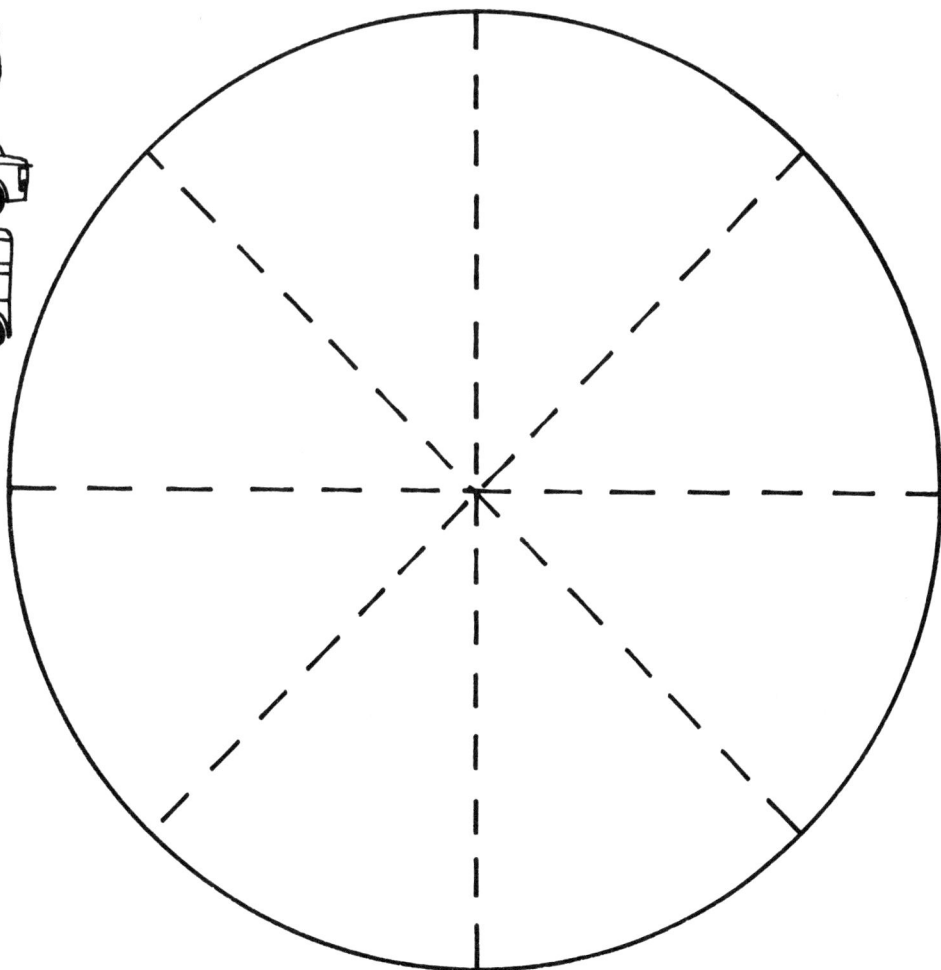

25

The High Street

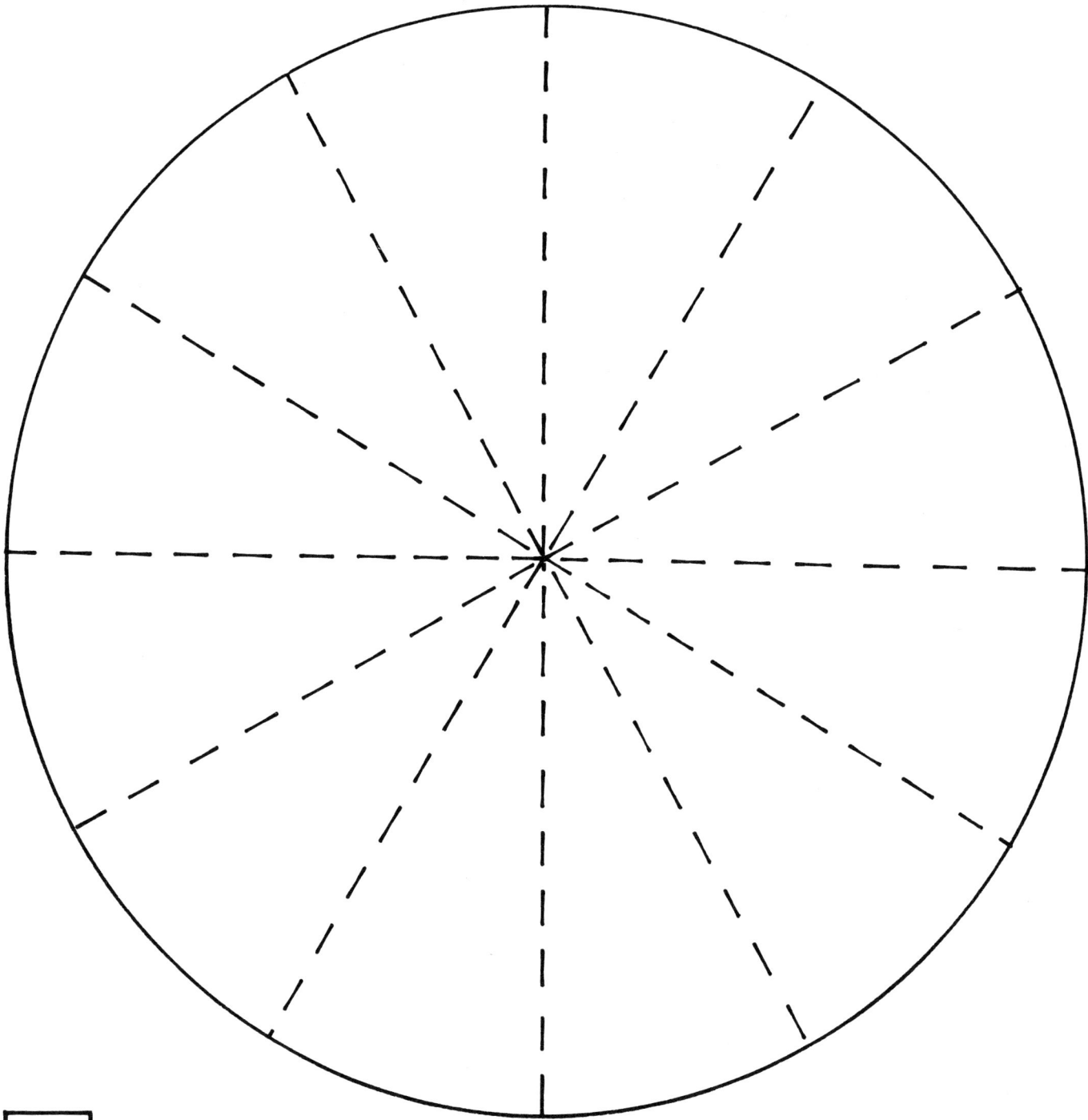

spring

summer

autumn

winter

The High Street

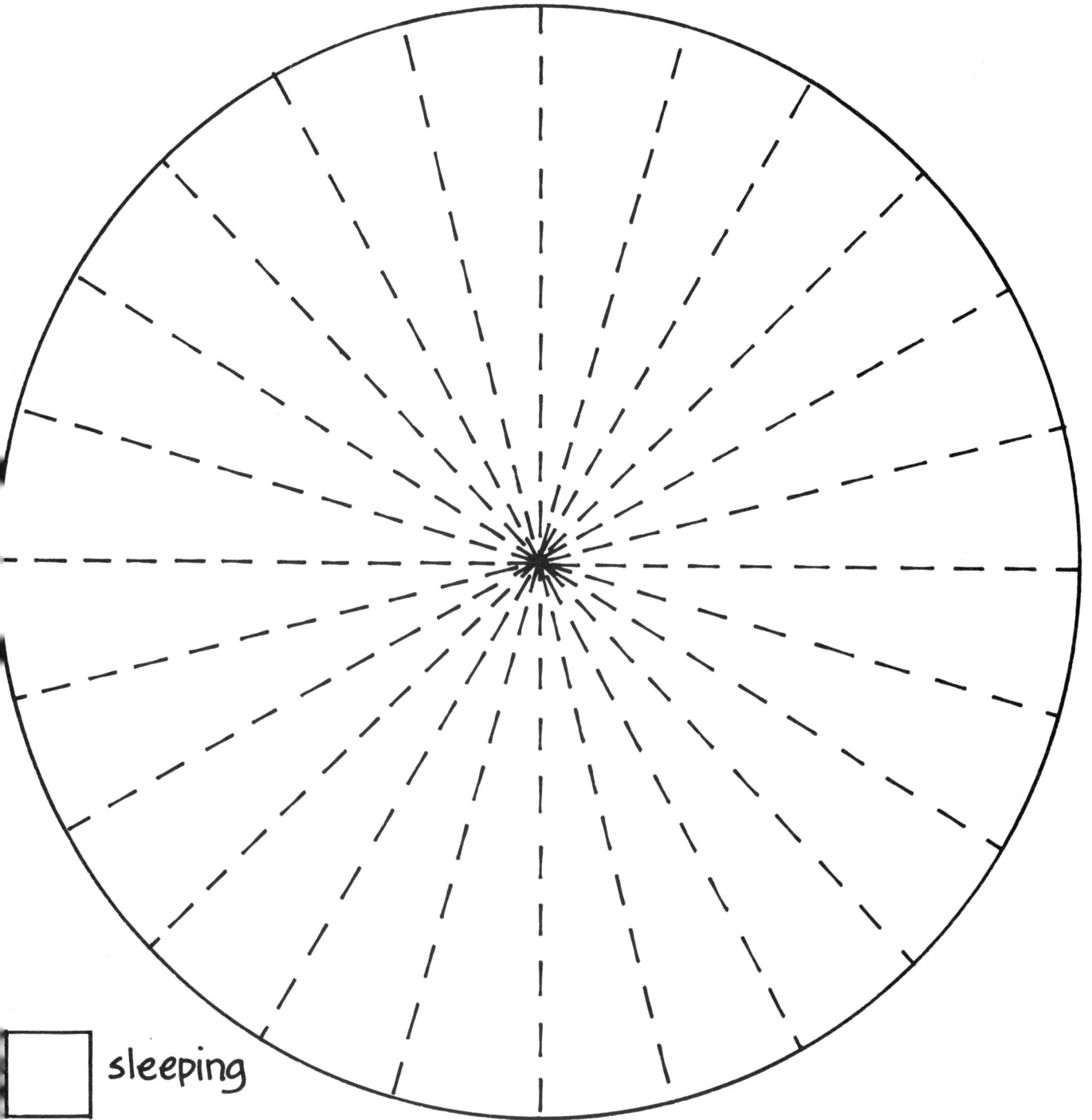

sleeping

eating

school

watching TV

other

Presenting

Pictograms

See photocopiable pages 30 to 32.

Objective

To create pictograms from observed and collected data.

Classroom development

Use the symbols and pictures on pages 30 to 32 to make pictograms of data that you have collected. Choose what the symbol should represent. For example:

represents 5 people

represents less than 5 people

Top of the Pops

The Chart Show

Neighbours

Grandstand

The ✗ symbol could represent a number of people, the car and the lorry may be useful for traffic surveys, the purse to record money collected. The sand timer could represent an amount of time. The television could represent the number of people who favour a TV programme or a number of hours of TV viewing.

Further activity

You may like to design some symbols of your own for pictograms and photocopy them for the chart.

Taller and taller

See photocopiable pages 33 and 34.

Objective

To create a bar line graph and to extrapolate.

Classroom development

Cut out the strips at the top of page 33. Place one alongside the first plant on page 34. Match the bottom of the strip with the soil level and mark the height of the plant on the strip. Cut off the surplus and stick the strip on to the graph on page 34 over the first dotted line. Continue for all eight pictures.

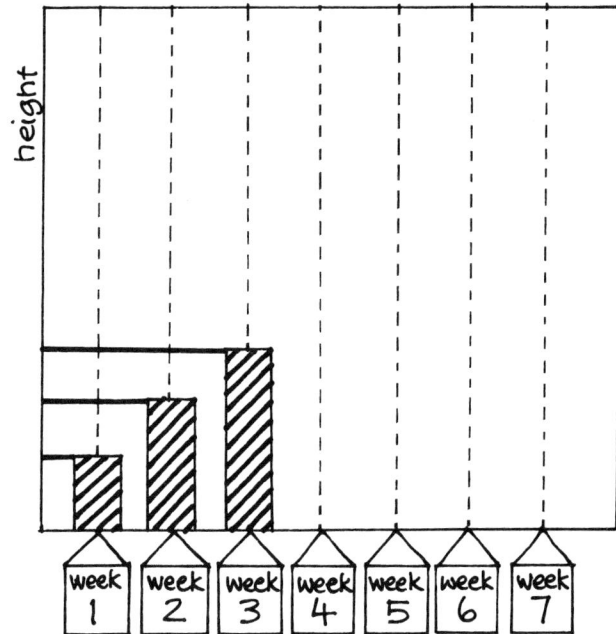

Draw a light pencil line from the top of each strip to the vertical axis. Estimate in which week the plant grew the most. Measure the distances marked on the vertical axis to check.

Predict what would happen to the plant's height in future weeks.

Further activities

Plant a seed of your own. Decide how frequently to measure the height of your plant. You may like to use thin paper strips or string. Make a bar line chart to show your plant's growth.

Changing times

See photocopiable page 35.

Objective

To create a simple conversion graph.

Classroom development

Use the grid on page 35 to make a graph to convert am/pm times to 24 hour times. Put a cross on the graph to match noon to 12.00 hours. Put a second cross on the graph to match another am/pm time to the 24 hour time. Join the points together with a straight pencil line. Extend the line to the origin (midnight/00.00) and as far as possible in the other direction.

Use the graph to help you convert times from a bus, railway, ferry or aeroplane timetable.

Further activities

Investigate time differences between Great Britain and cities such as Moscow and New York. Make a conversion graph using the grid on page 35.

Tour guide

See photocopiable pages 36 to 39.

Objectives

To convert distances on a map to real distances using a scale and a conversion graph. To convert kilometres to miles using a conversion graph. To plan an itinerary.

Classroom development

Imagine you are tour guide arranging a weekend break on the island on page 36. It is to be a family coach tour lasting from Friday to Sunday in the summer.

Investigate the distances between the places to visit on the map. Convert them to kilometres by completing and using the conversion graph on page 37.

The tourists would like to travel the full length of the coast road at some time over the weekend. They would also like to visit all of the attractions. They will need to spend more time at some than others. They are based at a hotel beside the beach and need to return there every night.

Plan an itinerary for their three day weekend on page 38.

The tour firm would like to know the miles travelled each day. You will therefore need to convert the kilometre distances to miles.

Use the grid on page 39. You will find two points already marked. Join them up to the

point (0,0) and extend the line as far as possible.

Use the conversion graphs to complete the itinerary.

Further activities

Investigate itineraries to find the shortest possible number of miles travelled.

Discover the fuel consumption of 50-seater coaches. Calculate the fuel that would be used if your itinerary were followed.

Shadows

See photocopiable page 40.

Objective

To create a curved line graph, and to interpolate from it.

Classroom development

Choose a short item such as a stick, pencil or a ruler. Place it upright outside on a sunny day. Measure the length of its shadow at regular time intervals and mark your results on to the grid on page 40. You may need to collect the data over several days.

Join the points into a curve. Estimate the height of the shadow at other times, using the curve.

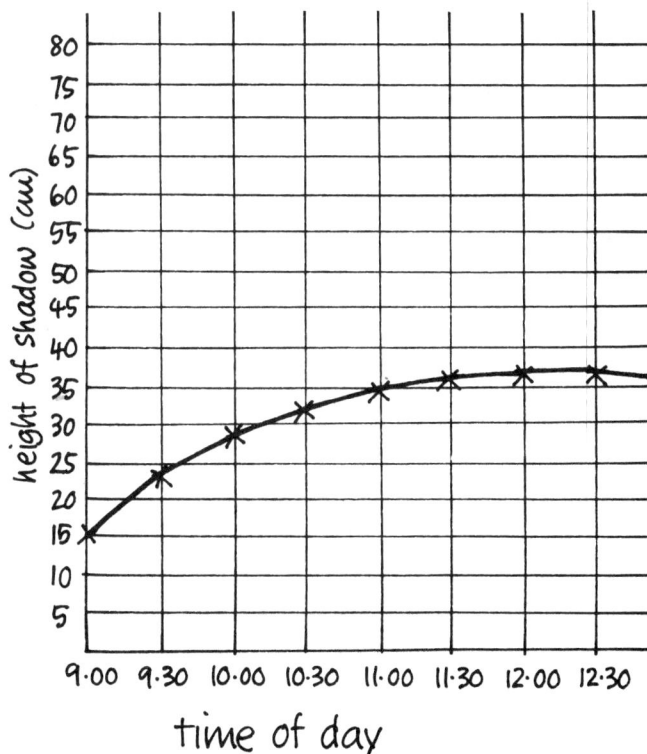

time of day

Further activities

Choose other, taller items and investigate shadows made by holding a torch at different angles.

Pictograms

Pictograms

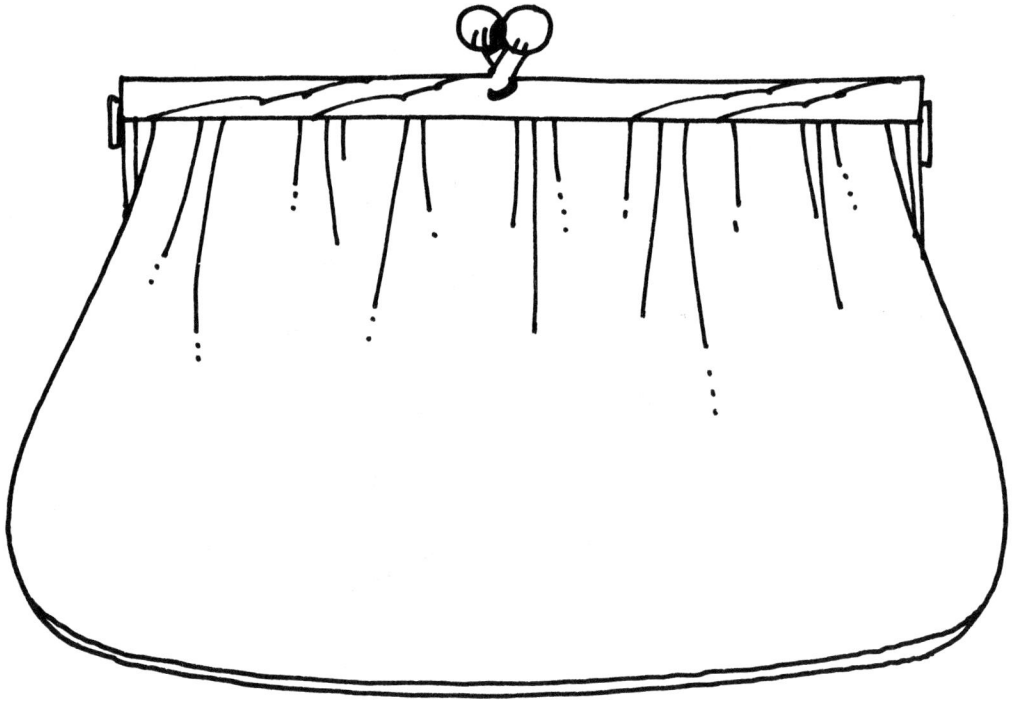

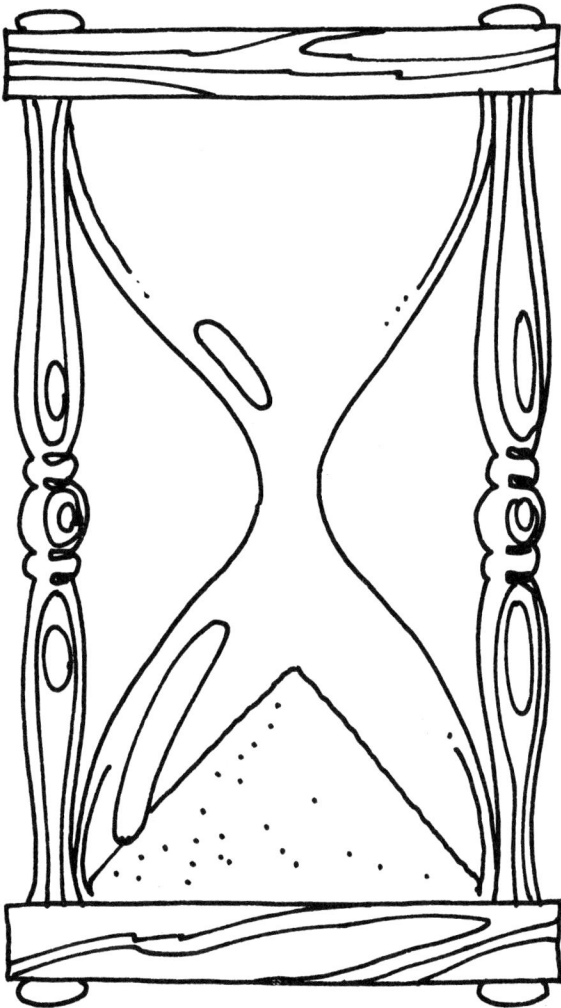

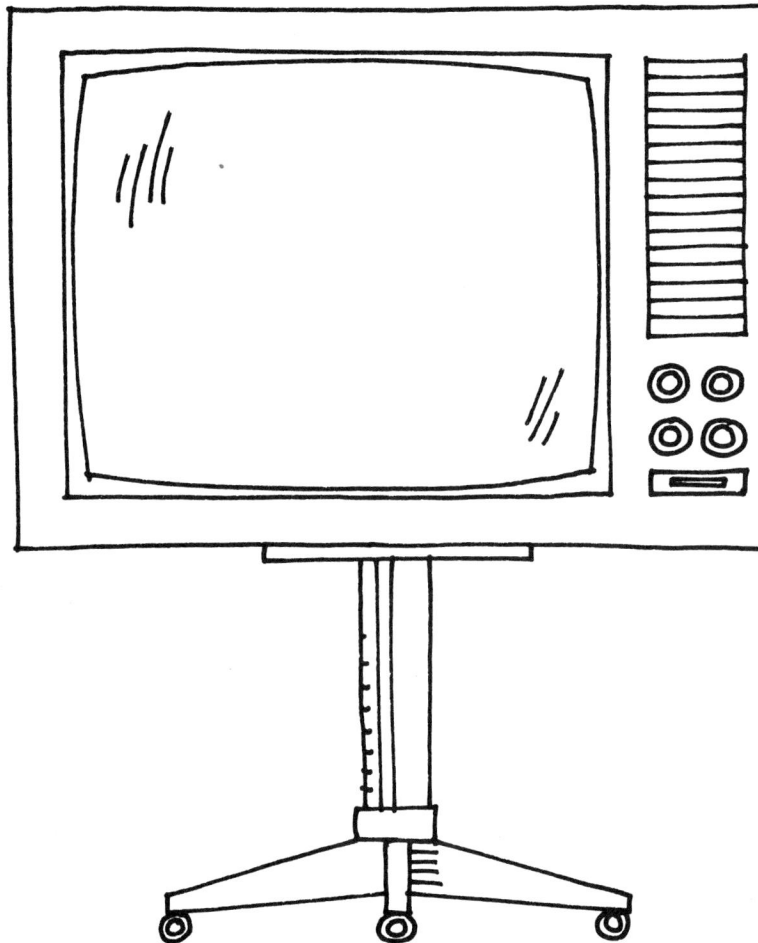

Taller and taller

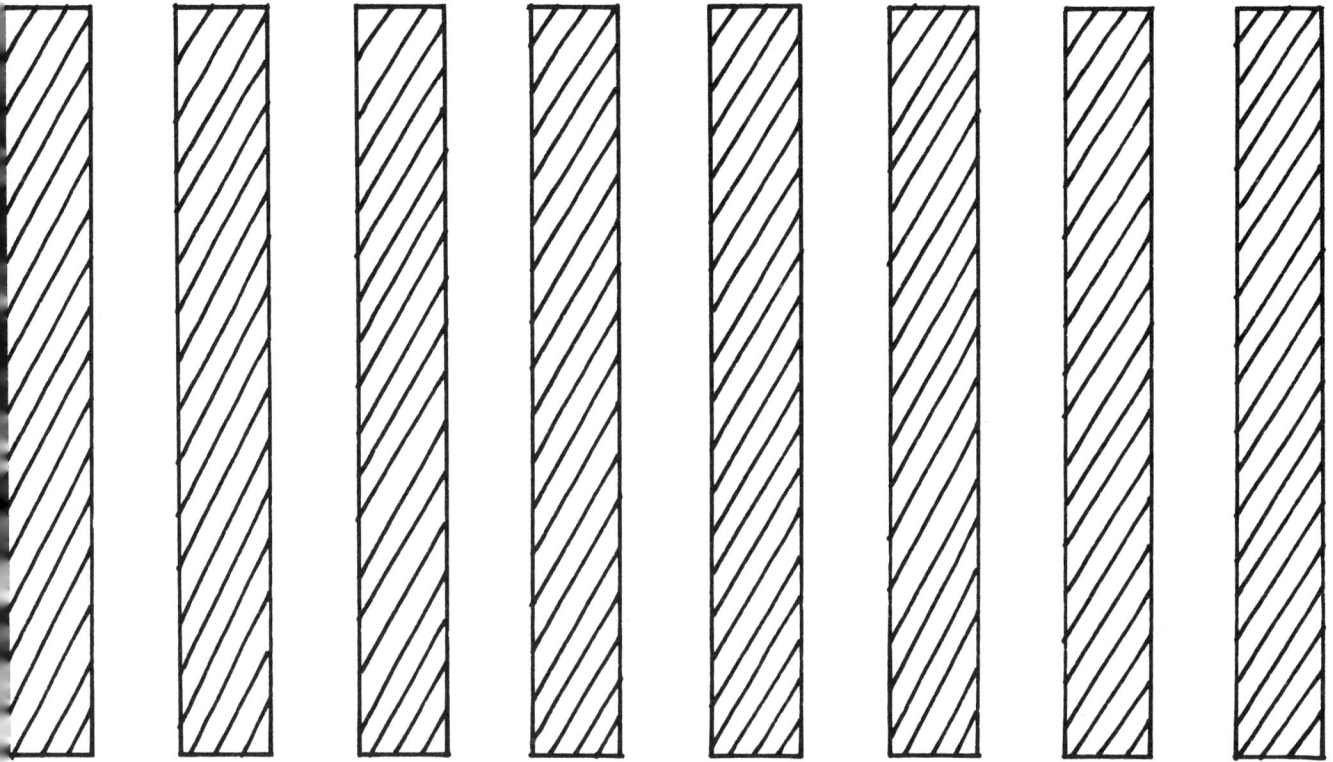

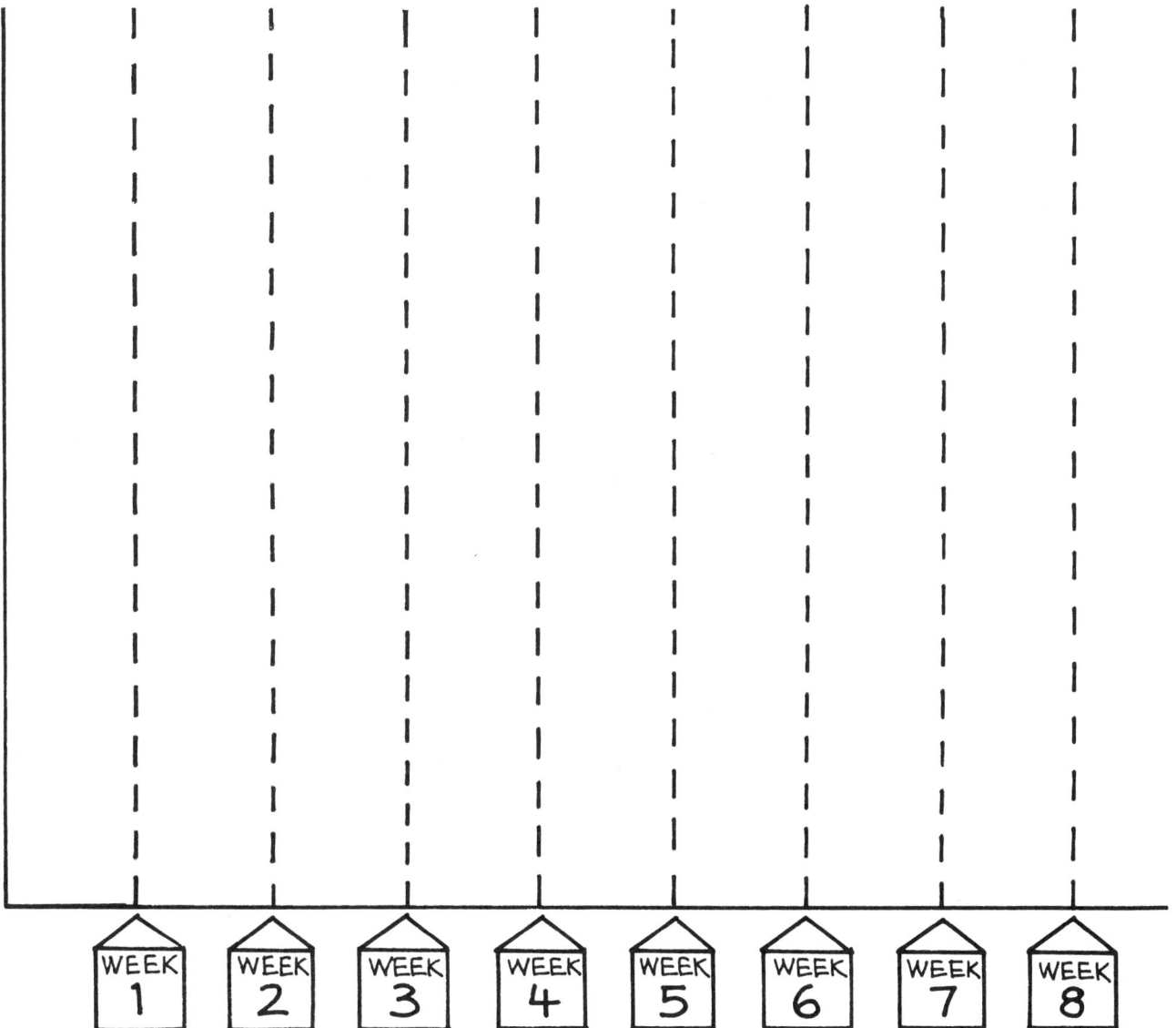

WEEK 1   WEEK 2   WEEK 3   WEEK 4   WEEK 5   WEEK 6   WEEK 7   WEEK 8

33

Taller and taller

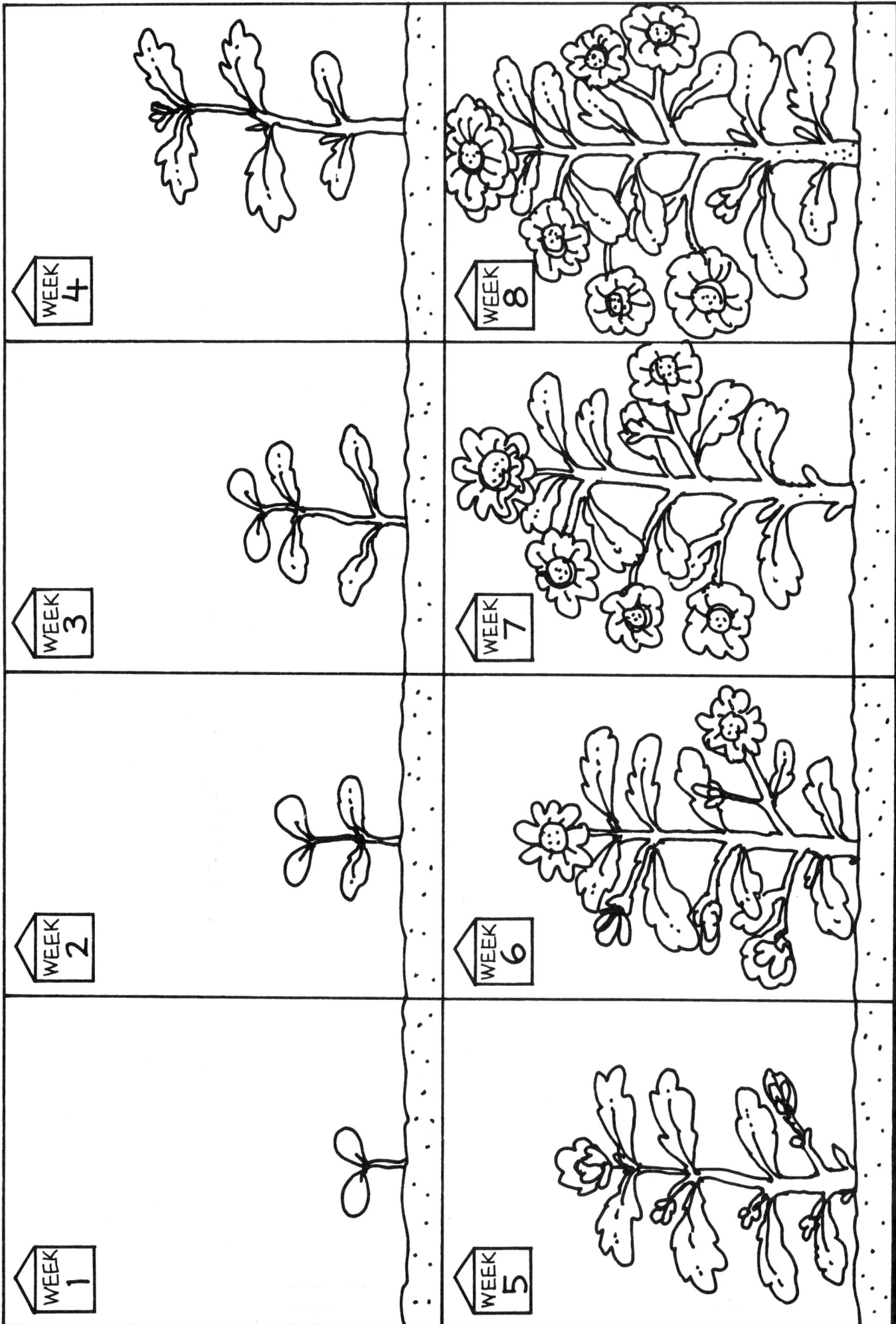

WEEK 4

WEEK 8

WEEK 3

WEEK 7

WEEK 2

WEEK 6

WEEK 1

WEEK 5

Changing times

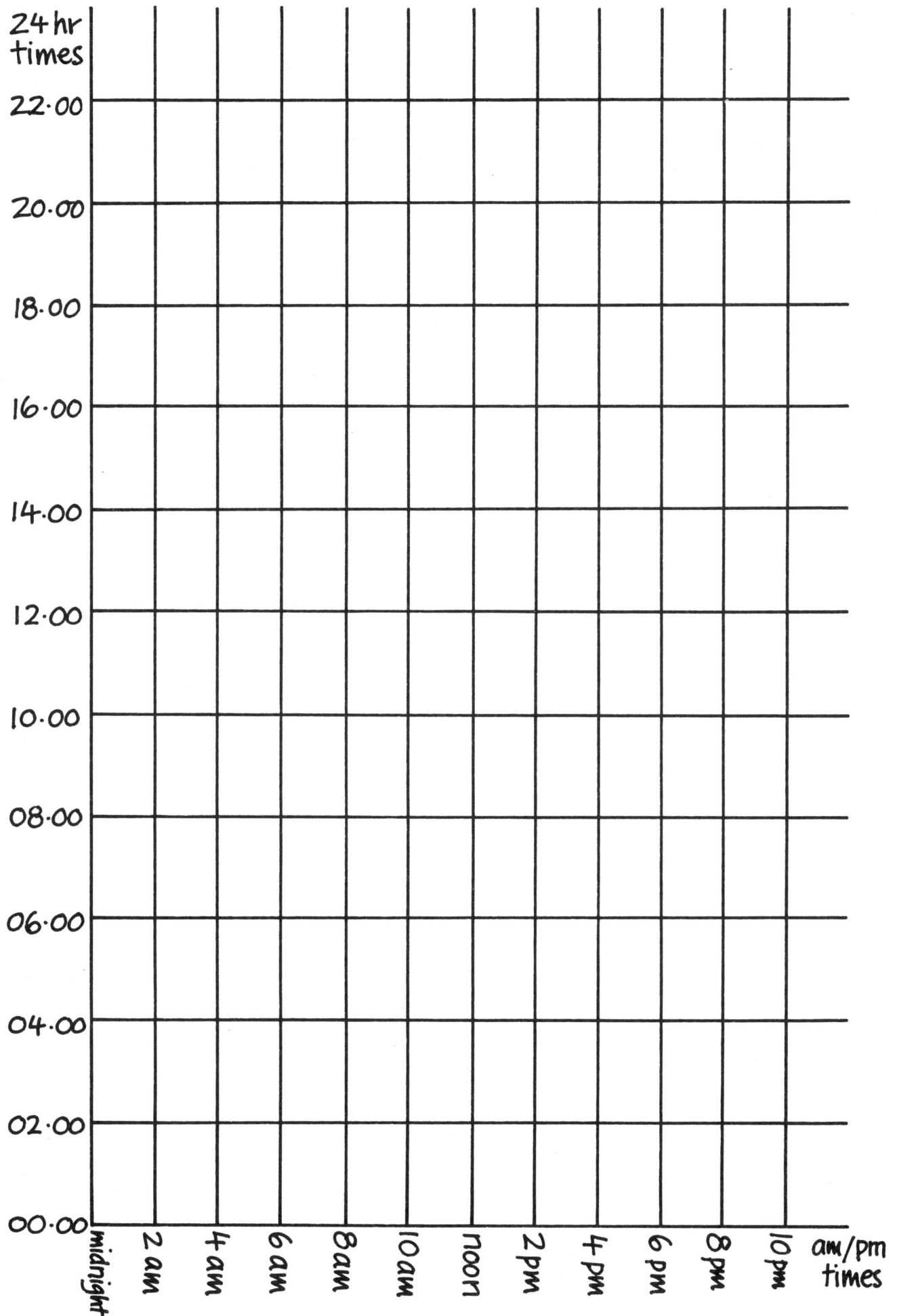

24 hr times	midnight	2 am	4 am	6 am	8 am	10 am	noon	2 pm	4 pm	6 pm	8 pm	10 pm	am/pm times
22·00													
20·00													
18·00													
16·00													
14·00													
12·00													
10·00													
08·00													
06·00													
04·00													
02·00													
00·00													

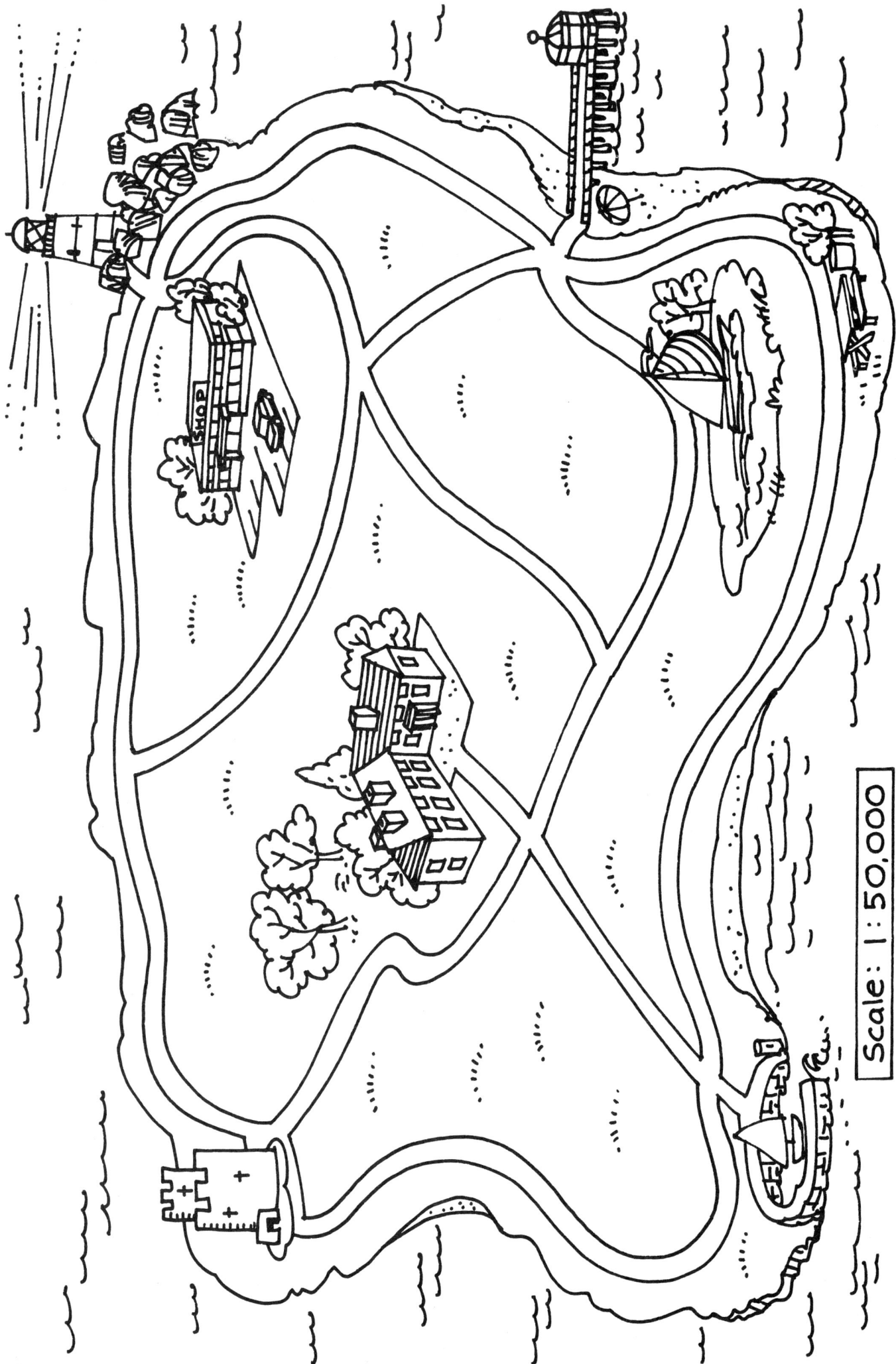

Tour guide

SHOP

Scale: 1 : 50,000

Tour guide

Actual distances

12 km
11 km
10 km
9 km
8 km
7 km
6 km
5 km
4 km
3 km
2 km
1 km

0   2 cm   4 cm   6 cm   7 cm   8 cm   9 cm   10 cm   11 cm   12 cm   13 cm   14 cm   15 cm

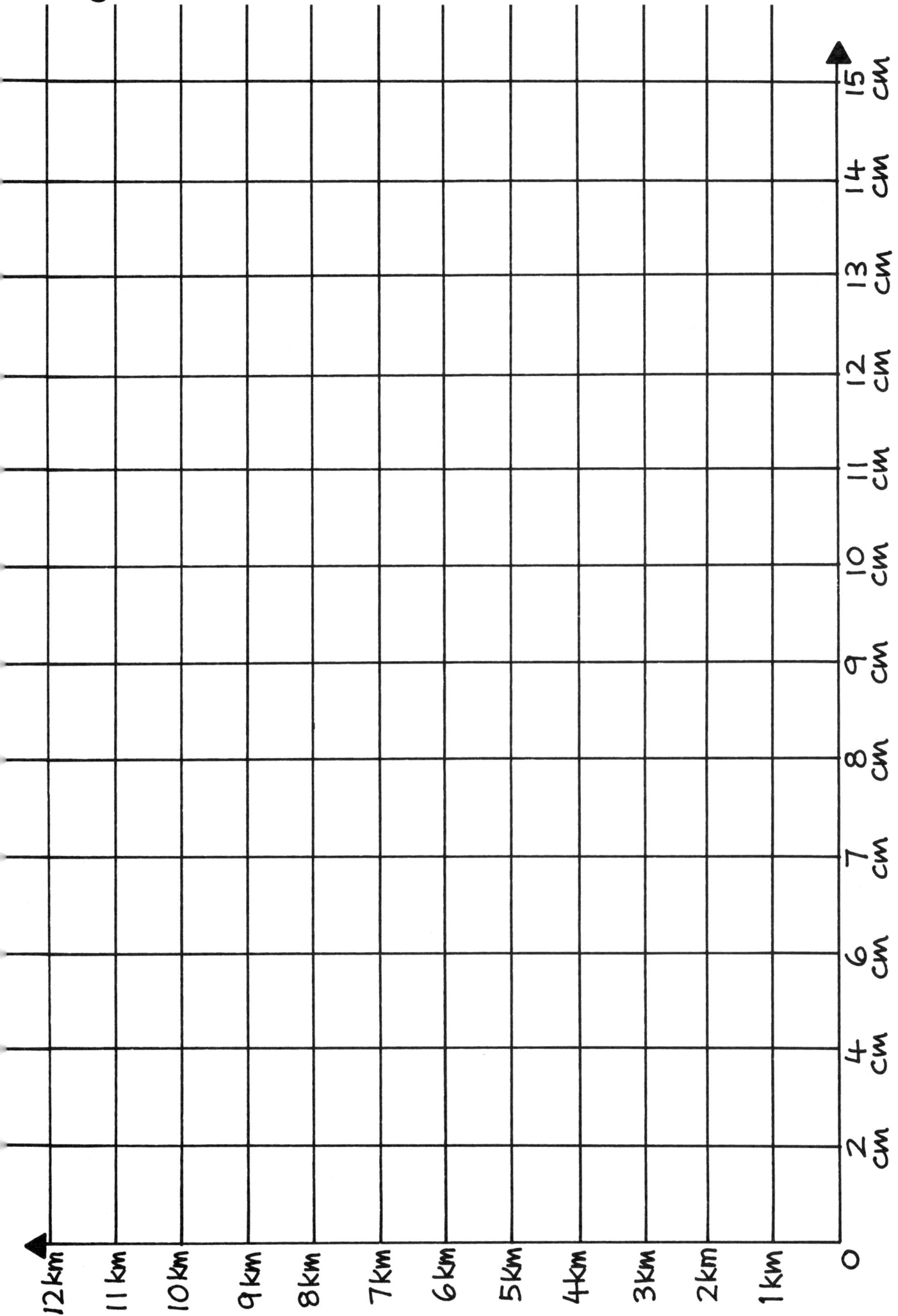

Distances on the map

Tour guide

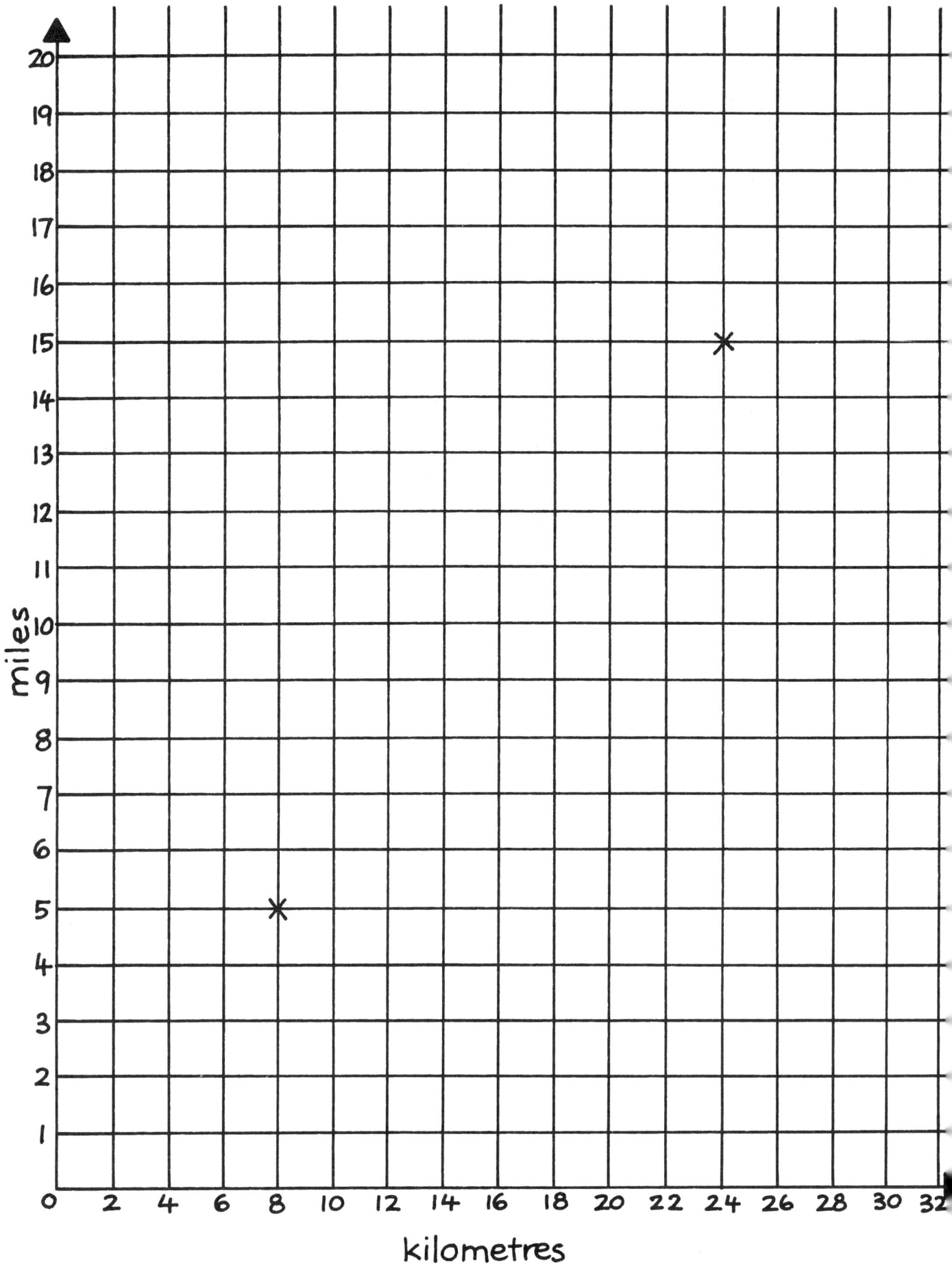

Tour guide

FRIDAY		
FROM	TO	MILES TRAVELLED
	TOTAL	

SATURDAY		
FROM	TO	MILES TRAVELLED
	TOTAL	

SUNDAY		
FROM	TO	MILES TRAVELLED
	TOTAL	

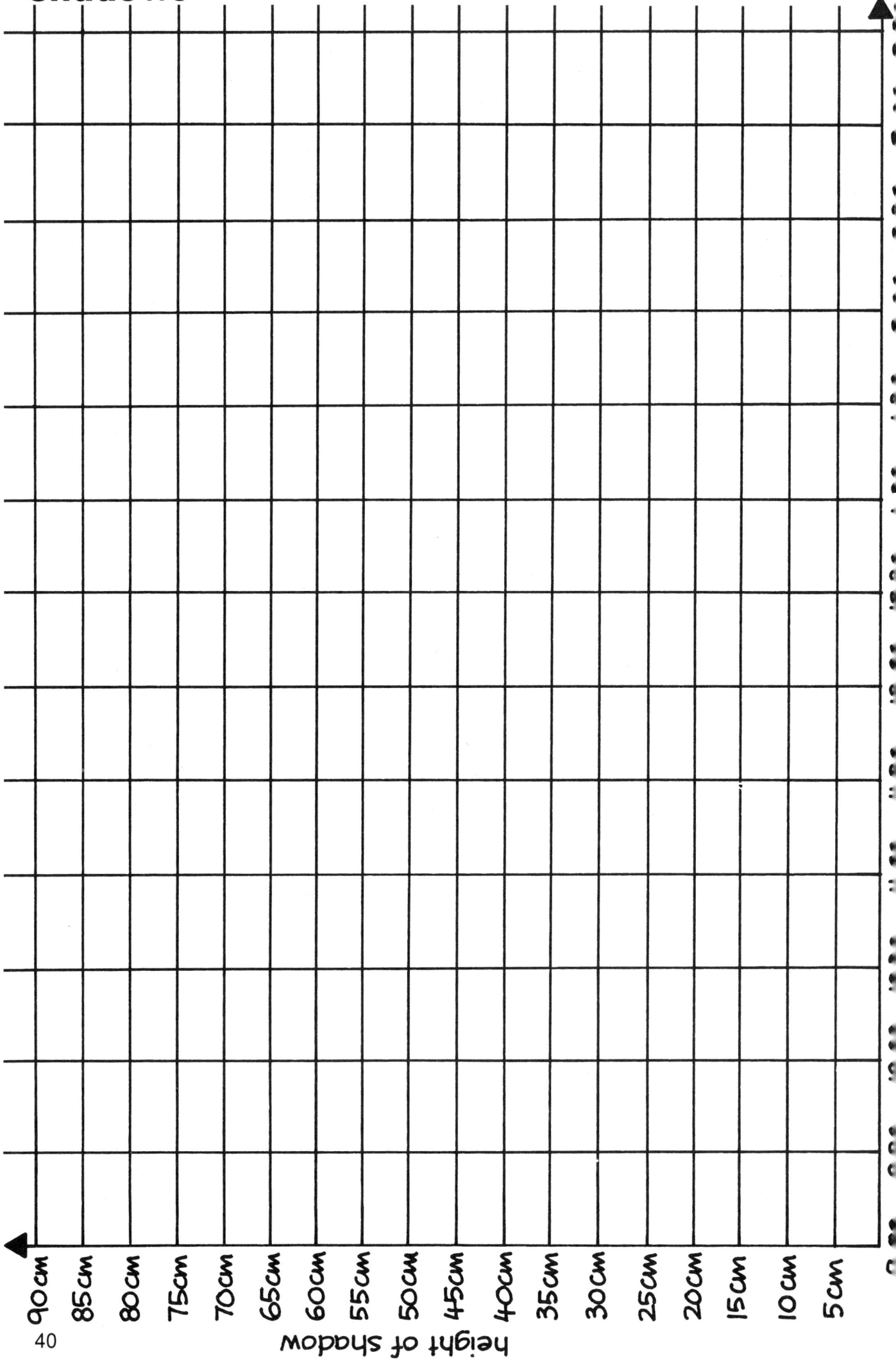

Shadows

height of shadow

90cm
85cm
80cm
75cm
70cm
65cm
60cm
55cm
50cm
45cm
40cm
35cm
30cm
25cm
20cm
15cm
10cm
5cm

Predicting

Butterflies

See photocopiable pages 43 to 45.

Objectives

To investigate simple probabilities including equally likely events, and to investigate the range of possible outcomes of combined events.

Classroom development

Make the spinner at the bottom of page 43 or

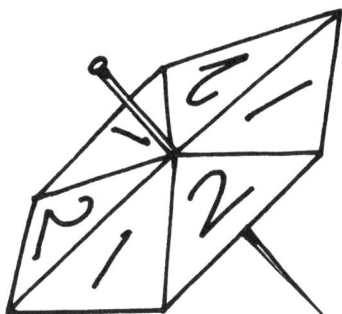

use a six-sided die marked with ones and twos. Play the game with a friend. You will need one copy each of pages 43 and 44. Take it in turns to spin the spinner and cut out the appropriate number of wings from page 43. Stick the wings on to a butterfly outline on page 44. Continue until you have completed a butterfly with four wings. Move on to a new outline if you have five wings. Stick the extra wing into the square beside the butterfly and move on to a new outline. Play continues until one player has completed twelve butterflies.

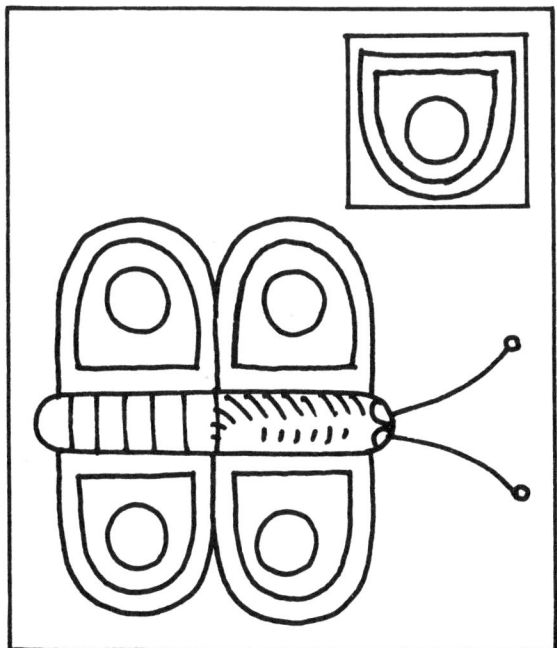

Count how many times you managed to win four wings and five wings. Did your friend achieve similar results? Do you think there is an equal chance of getting four and five wings?

What is the probability of spinning a one or a two? What is the probability of spinning two ones consecutively?

Look at the probability tree on page 45. Complete the first spin column by filling in the number of wings possible to win after one go. Continue to the second spin column. How many different number of wings is it possible to have won at this stage?

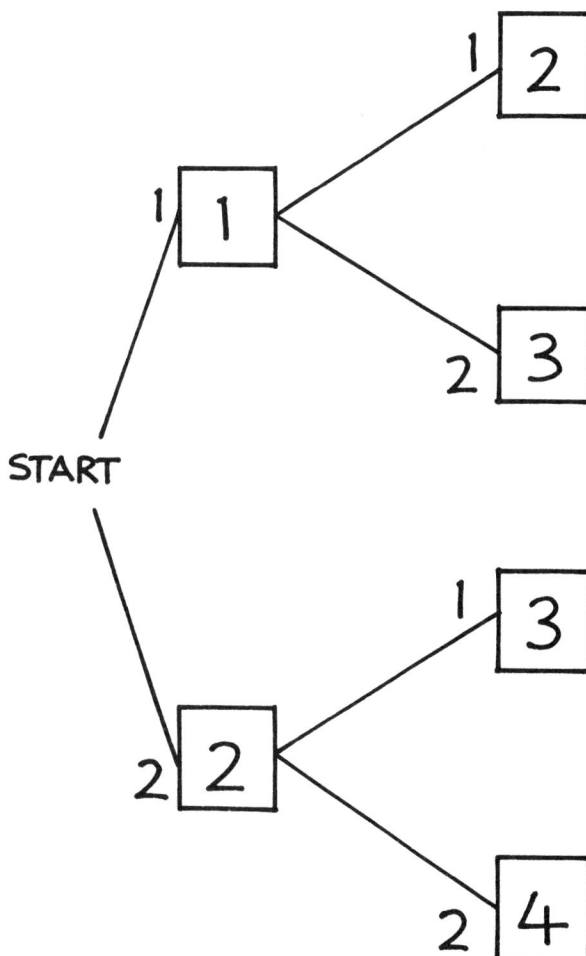

What is the probability of having completed a butterfly after two spins?

Continue to the third and fourth spin columns. How many different ways are there to win four wings? How many ways are there to win five wings? Which event is the most likely? Compare with your own results.

Further activities

Make a spinner marked 1, 2, 3 or use a 1 to 3 die, and investigate possible totals after one, two and three throws. Make a probability tree.

Families

See photocopiable pages 46 to 48.

Objective

To investigate simple probabilities of combined events, and to investigate all possible outcomes.

Classroom development

Join pages 47 and 48 together with sticky

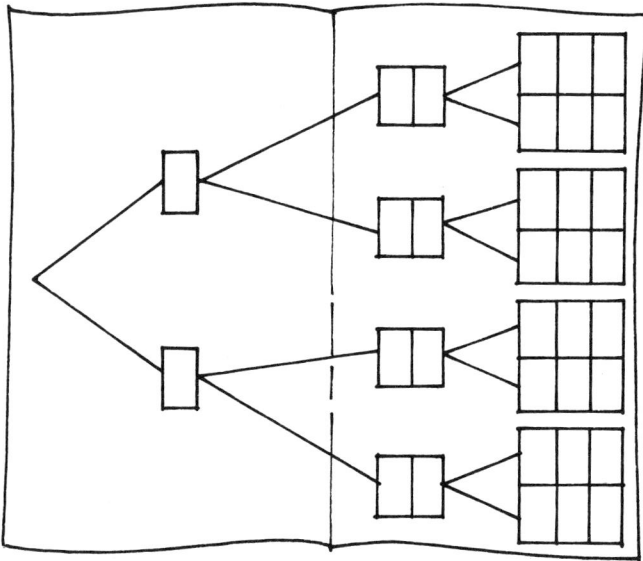

tape so that the lines match. Look at the first column of the probability tree. It indicates the possibilities for a one child family. Cut out a boy and a girl symbol from page 46 and stick them into the spaces in the first column.

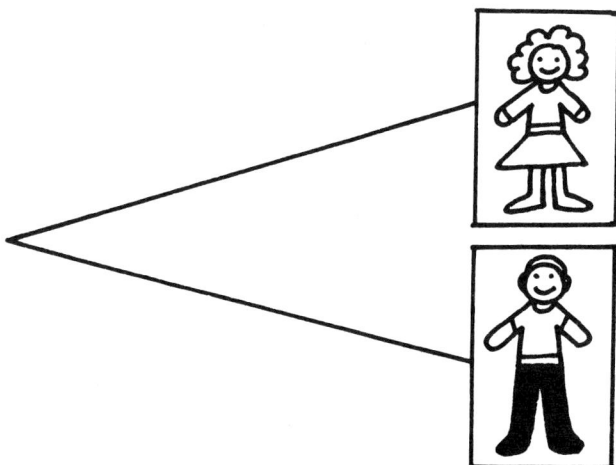

If the family then decides to have another child, what is the probability of them having a girl or a boy? If they already have one girl what is the probability of them having another girl? Complete the second column by sticking down the symbols to represent all the possible families with two children.

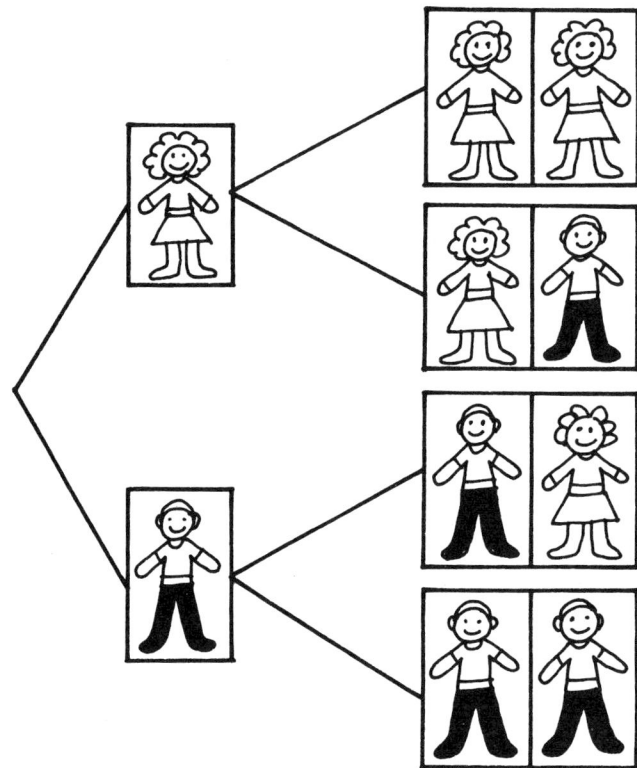

What is the probability of having two children of the same sex? What is the probability of having at least one girl?

Complete the third column. What is the probability of having three children of the same sex? What is the probability of having two boys? What is the probability of having at least one boy? What is the probability of the first child being a boy, the second being a girl and the third being a boy?

Further activities

Make a survey of the families of your class and the two other classes. Compare them with your probability tree. Continue it further if necessary. Does your survey support your prediction?

Butterflies

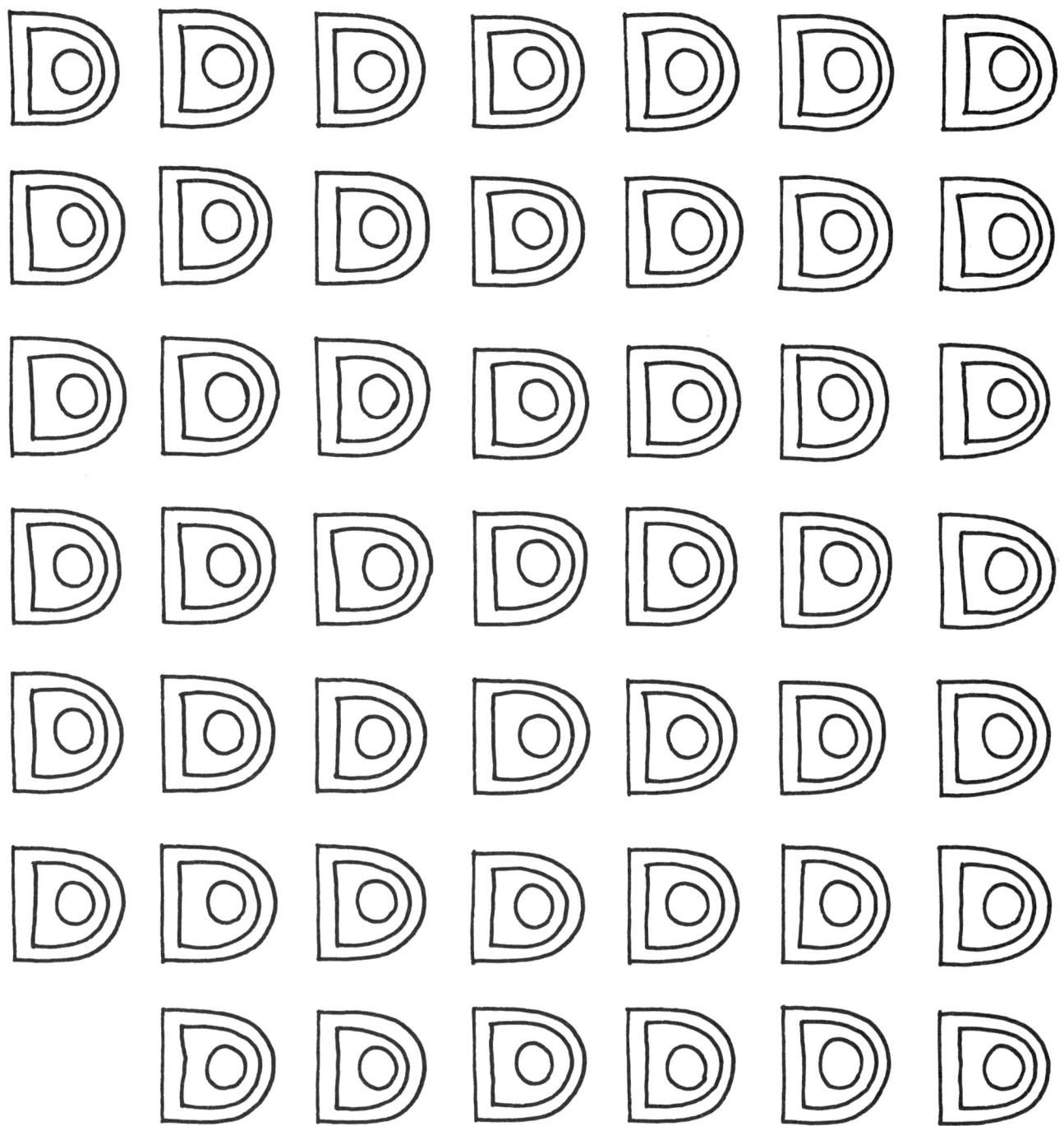

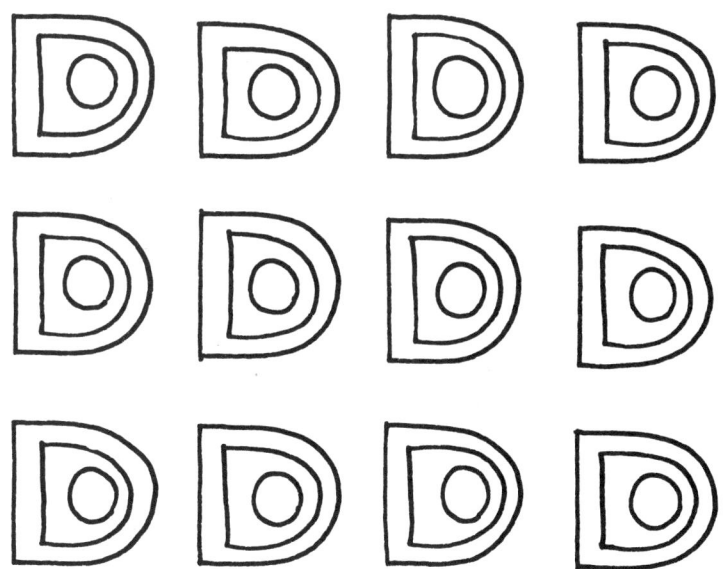

Butterflies

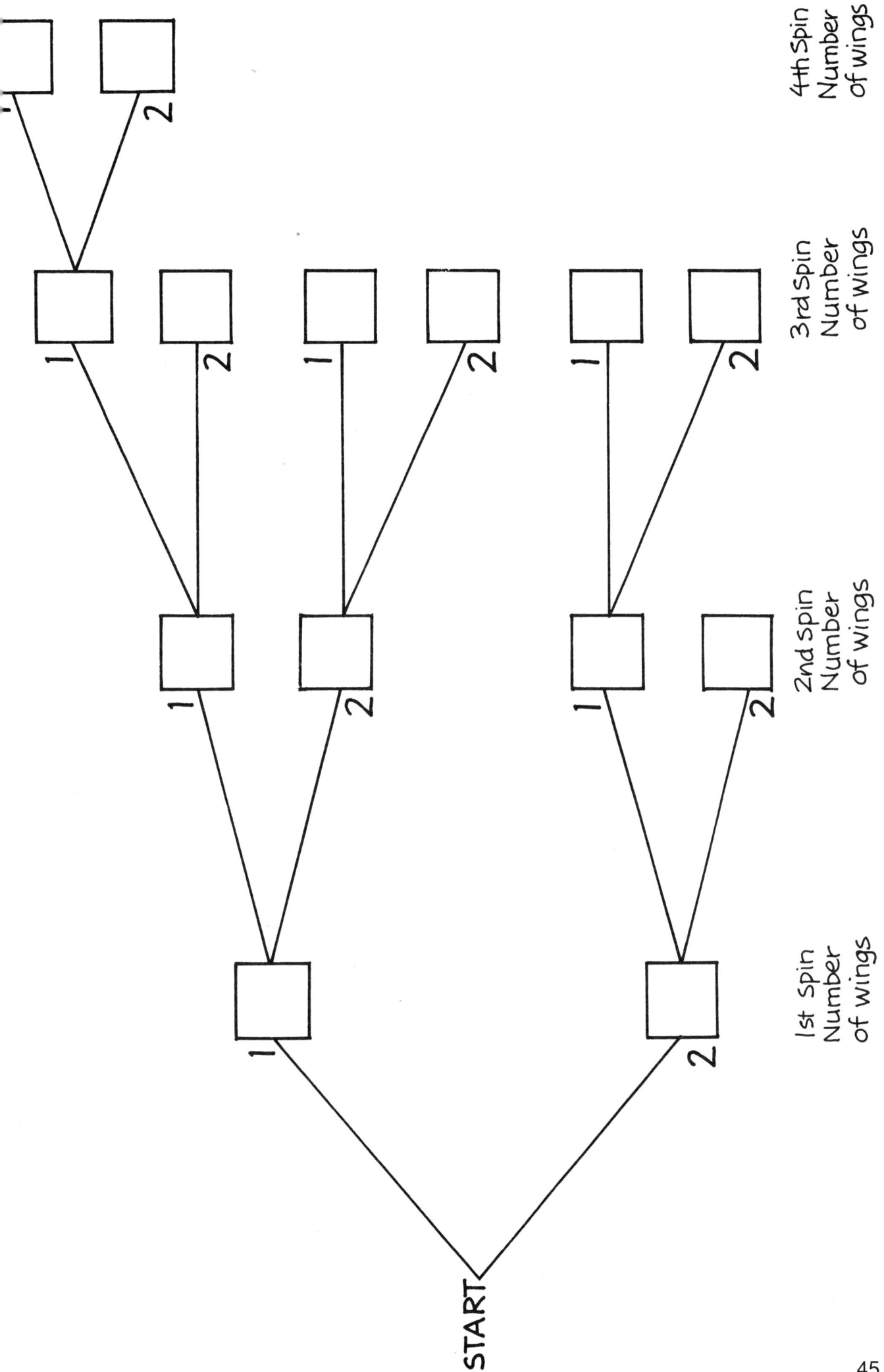

Butterflies

START

1st Spin
Number
of wings

1   2

2nd Spin
Number
of wings

1   2   1   2

3rd Spin
Number
of wings

1   2   1   2   1   2

4th Spin
Number
of wings

1   2

45

Families

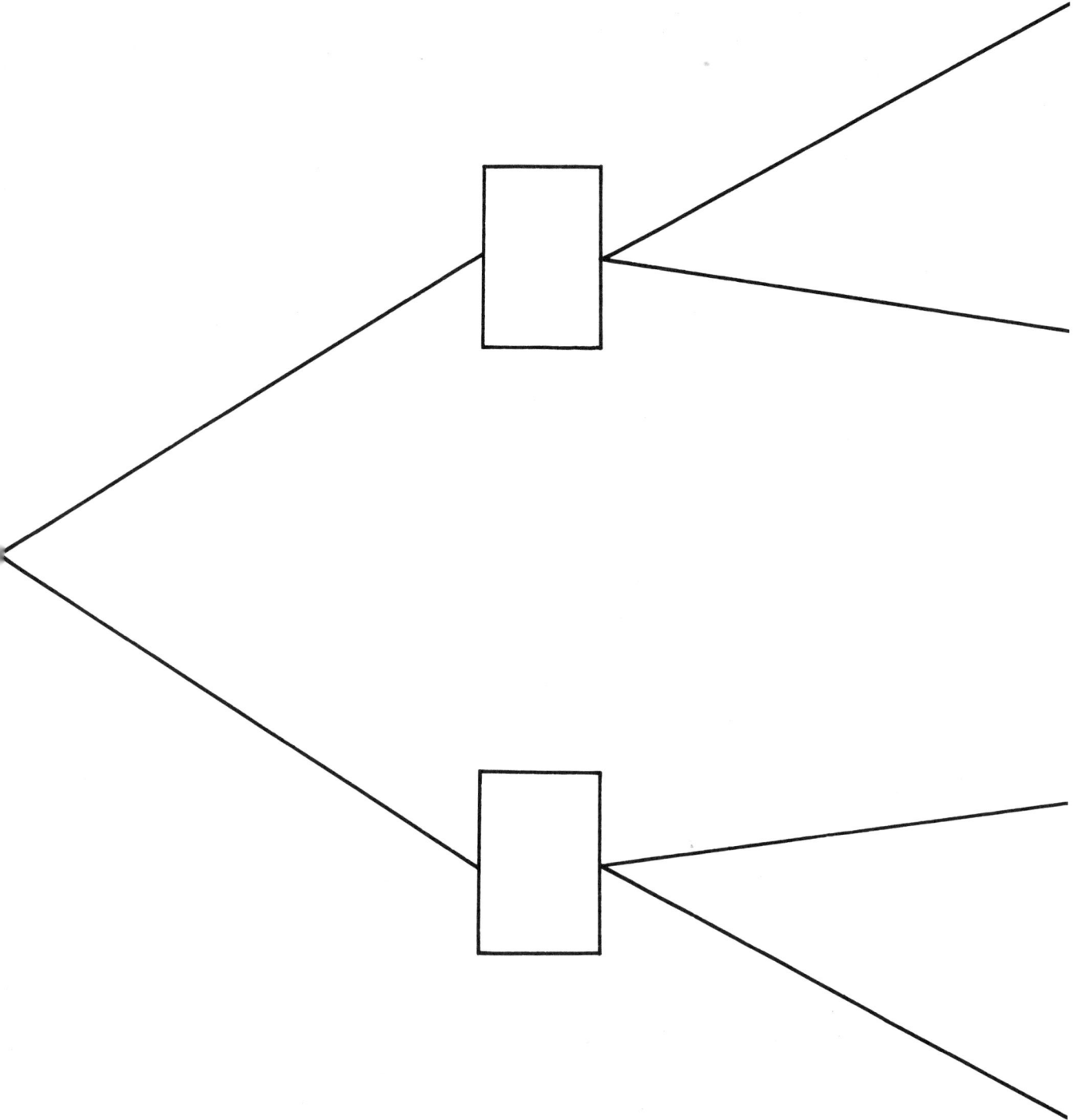

Families

Families

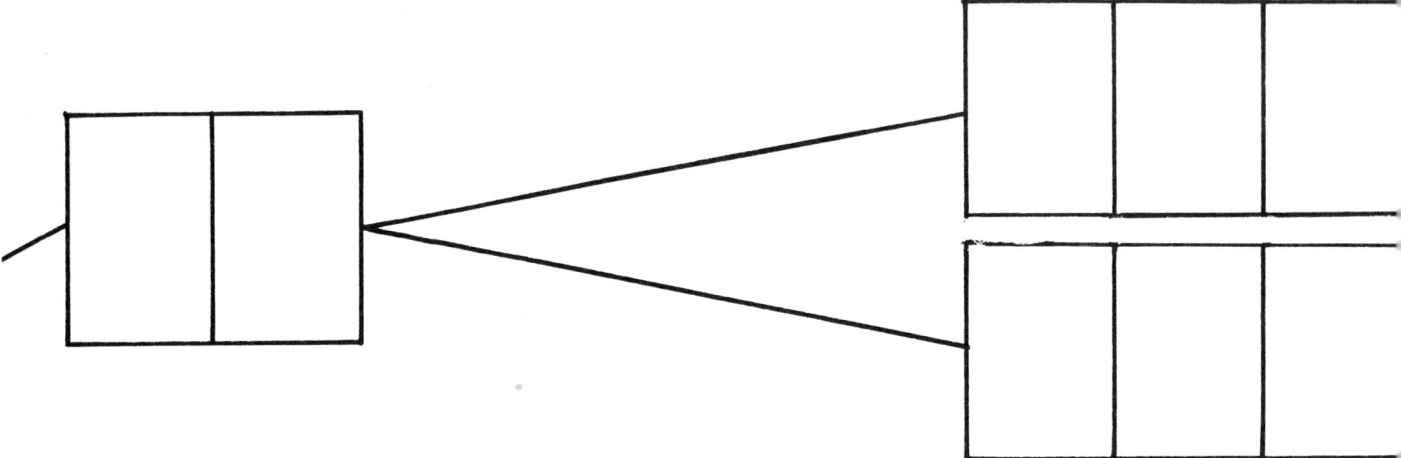

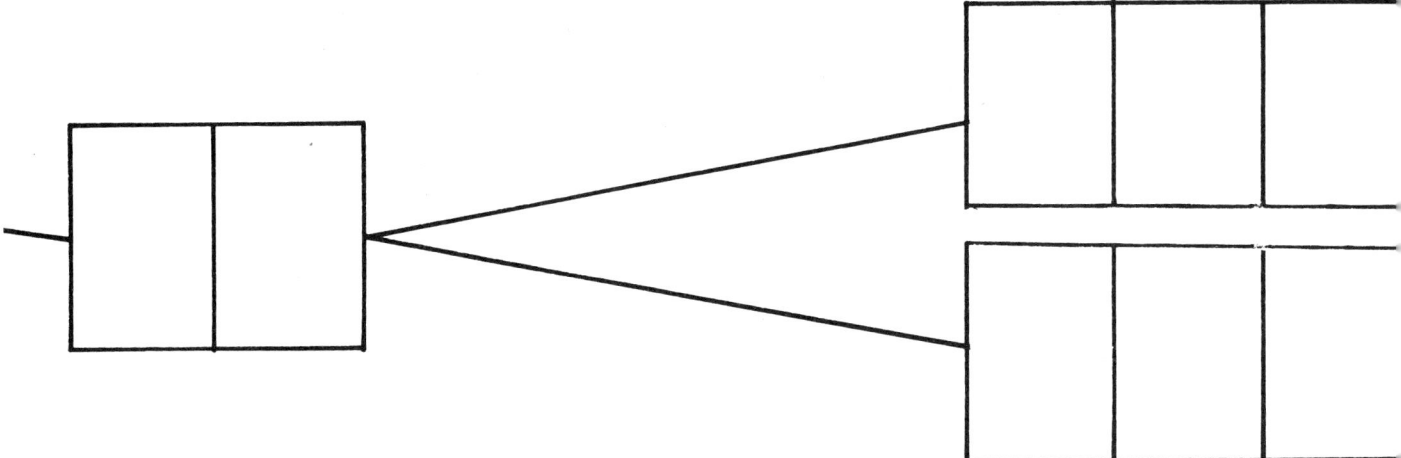

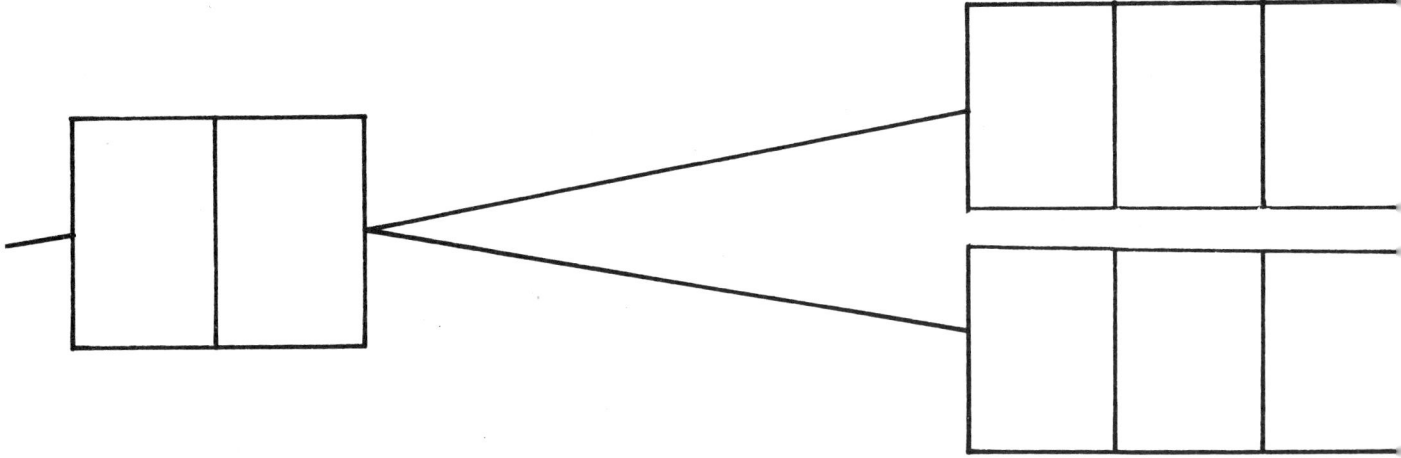

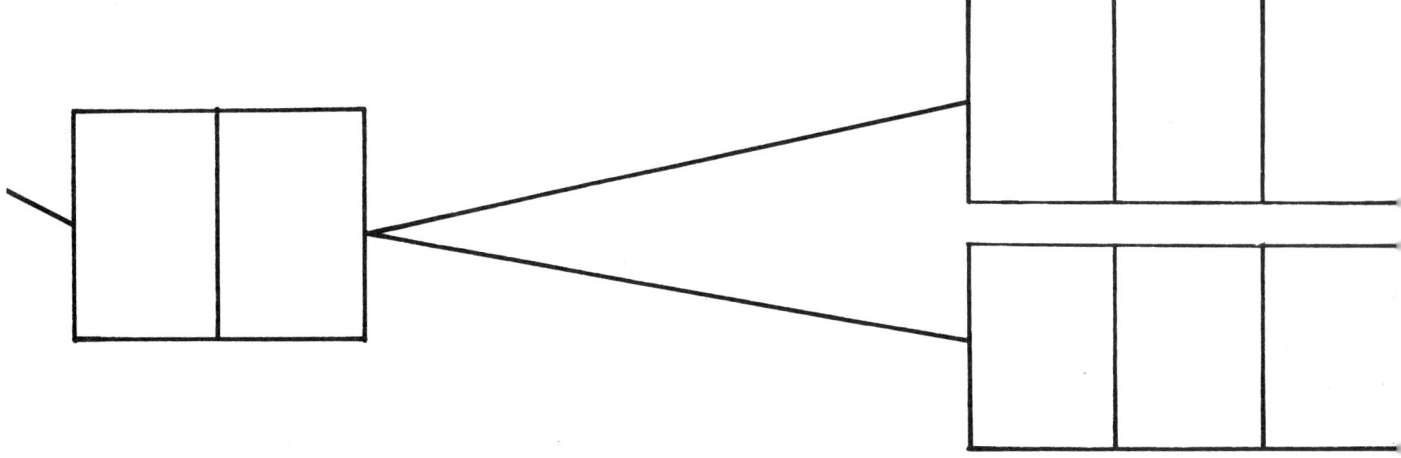